From Chaos to Calm: An A to Z Playbook to Create Positive Behavior Transformations in Children.

Gwendolyn A. Martin, Ed.D., LPC

Also by Dr. Gwen D.E.A.R Journal

(Drop Everything And Reflect)

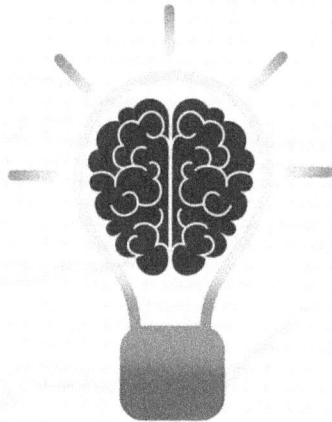

D.E.A.R
Journal
Drop Everything And Reflect

GWENDOLYN A. MARTIN, ED.D, LPC

This book is dedicated to ALL who aspire to help children EXPLORE, EXPRESS, and REGULATE their emotions in fun and creative ways.

Contents

Introduction

As parents, educators, caregivers, and counselors, we all share the goal of helping children grow into emotionally balanced, confident, and kind individuals. Yet, guiding children (and adults) through emotional and behavioral challenges can often feel endless and overwhelming, leaving us exhausted, frustrated, and questioning how to respond effectively. From Chaos to Calm: An A to Z Playbook of Behavioral Transformations in Children was born out of a desire to provide a practical, easy-to-use guide for those who support children on a daily basis. As I began to develop the outline for this book, I vividly remembered a conversation with a school administrator in which I was asked if I could produce notes on managing classroom behaviors to help others. As I transitioned into private practice and started a mental health and educational consulting business, I realized that managing challenging behaviors, especially in young children, often caused significant chaos for many people at home and in school. After all, we were dealing with the impact of the COVID-19 pandemic, where routine and structure were often not expected or required. As a result, I frequently receive requests to work with kids, parents, and educators to teach behavior management and emotional regulation in children and the adults who care for them.

Why This Book?

After years of working with children, families, and educators as a special education teacher, school counselor, school administrator, and licensed professional counselor, I have seen firsthand how behavior is often misunderstood. What looks like defiance may be frustration, what appears to be laziness may be a sign of being overwhelmed, and what seems like attention-seeking may be a genuine need for connection. I wrote this book to bridge the gap between challenges and solutions, offering a compassionate, step-by-step approach to fostering positive behavior.

This book is a structured playbook from A to Z, making it an easy-to-read, practical go-to guide for understanding, addressing, and correcting common behavioral challenges at home and school. Each chapter focuses on key behavioral concepts, providing:

- Practical tips, tools, and compelling research-based strategies to guide children through behavioral struggles.
- Insights into the "why" behind behaviors while helping adults respond with empathy and grace instead of frustration.
- Step-by-step interventions for transforming challenging moments into teachable opportunities.
- Real-life examples and scenarios to illustrate how to apply these strategies and interventions in daily life.
- Self-reflection questions and prompts to help parents, educators, caregivers, and practitioners manage their own emotional responses while supporting children.

The Benefits of This Book

By using the strategies in this playbook, you will:

- Feel more confident in handling behavioral challenges with patience and understanding.
- Help children develop emotional regulation skills to understand and manage their feelings and actions.
- Strengthen your connection with children by fostering trust and open communication.
- Discover how to remain calm in challenging moments, transforming chaos into opportunities for growth.
- Create a calm, inviting, positive, and structured environment that fosters children's behavioral, social, and emotional growth.

The Journey Begins

Whether you are a parent, teacher, caregiver, or counselor, this book is designed to be your companion in guiding children from chaos to calm. The path to positive behavior transformation isn't easy. It doesn't happen overnight, but meaningful, lasting change is possible with the right tools, patience, and a heart full of love, kindness, grace, and understanding.

Let's take this journey together, one step, one strategy, one day, and one transformed behavior at a time. You are not alone!

Parenting & Teaching with Purpose:

Patience, Growth, and Guiding with Love

Today is a day of transformation. We will begin with a promise letter to help you set your intentions for patience, growth, and love as you embark on the journey from chaos to calm. I want to help you move from feeling overwhelmed and alone to feeling empowered and supported. First, I need you to trust the process to transform your child's or your student's behavior. I won't lie and tell you that navigating the storm will be easy. However, I can assure you that giving yourself grace, using failure as an opportunity for growth, guiding with love, and utilizing the tools and strategies in this A to Z playbook will yield positive results. Remember, every small step counts and gets you closer to your desired goal. YOU can WIN!

Writing a promise letter is empowering. It can improve your mood, reduce stress and anxiety, provide accountability, and increase your likelihood of success. It will also serve as a personal reminder to stay grounded, embrace growth, and lead with patience and calmness, even in the most challenging moments. It is a powerful way to reaffirm your commitment to transforming behaviors (yours and the child's) while reflecting on the journey from chaos to calm.

As you begin writing, take a moment to reflect on why you decided NOW is the time to make a change. Be open, honest, transparent, and nonjudgmental of your feelings, ideas, hopes, and dreams as they surface. Get it all out, release, and let go! After completing this playbook, as you continue your journey, look back and reflect on the progression, challenges, and triumphs.

Here are a few suggestions to get you started:

1. **Find a quiet corner** where you can reflect free of distractions. Then, take a few deep, calming breaths and consider your role in shaping children's behavior and emotions.

2. **Begin with a warm and encouraging greeting**, as if you are writing to a beloved friend or family member. A greeting as simple as "Dear [Your Name]" is a good place to start.

3. **Acknowledge the challenges and your commitment to growth.** Now is a good time to recognize your parenting or teaching difficulties. Acknowledge that behavior transformation doesn't happen overnight and that children (and adults) do better when they know better. For example: "I know transforming behavior from chaos to calm is not going to be easy. There will be tough days, but I'm up for the challenge and will face adversity with patience, understanding, and love.

4. **Set your intentions for patience, growth, and guidance with love.** Write about how you will approach challenges with patience, embrace growth opportunities, and use love and understanding as the foundation for change. For example: "I promise to freeze before reacting, to take a calming breath before responding, and to

remind myself that every moment is an opportunity for growth, not just for the children I guide, but for myself, as well.

5. **Acknowledge your own emotions and self-care.** Recognize that your needs matter, too, and are vital to supporting children effectively. Example: "I will practice self-care daily to show up as the best version of ME. I will give myself grace on hard days and remember to celebrate the small victories."

6. **Encourage yourself with affirmations.** Close your letter with encouragement by offering a final affirmation. Example: "I am capable. I am strong. I am determined to make a positive change. I choose to lead with love, patience, and purpose. And no matter what today brings, I will show up with kindness for myself and the children in my care."

7. **Sign and date your letter.** By signing and dating your letter, you are adding a layer of accountability. Your signature makes your commitment feel real and personal. Revisit your promise whenever you need encouragement and a reminder to keep pushing. You got this!

~ My Promise ~

~ My Promise ~

A

All behavior is
communication.
The question is,
are we listening?

A – Antecedents, Behaviors, and Consequences (ABCs)

Understanding why inappropriate and disruptive behaviors occur is the foundation of meaningful behavior transformation. **The ABC Model, comprising Antecedents (what happens before the behavior), Behaviors (observable actions), and Consequences (what happens after the behavior),** is a robust, evidence-based framework that can be used by educators, parents, counselors, and caregivers to observe, understand, and shape behavior. When we take time to observe the ABCs of behavior, we can shift from reacting to challenging moments to **responding with intention**. The ABC model empowers adults to support behavioral transformation by creating environments and routines that teach children better ways to cope, express themselves, and succeed.

Antecedents ("triggers")

Antecedents are the events, actions, or circumstances that occur immediately before a behavior. They serve as triggers or cues that lead to specific responses. By identifying and adjusting antecedents, adults can proactively prevent challenging behaviors. Prevention might involve modifying the environment, changing the way instructions are given, or providing clear expectations.

Examples:

- A loud noise or a chaotic classroom environment
- Being asked to complete a difficult task or an unpreferred activity
- A transition between activities or settings
- Another child taking a toy

Behaviors

Behavior refers to the specific, observable action the child performs. The behavior should be described clearly and objectively, without assumptions or emotional bias. Focusing on what the child actually **does** (rather than what we assume they're feeling or intending) allows for more precise analysis and more effective intervention strategies.

Examples:

- Hitting, kicking, biting, and throwing objects
- Crying, yelling, screaming, cursing, or inappropriate language
- Refusing to follow directions

Consequences

Consequences are the results or outcomes that follow a behavior. They can either increase or decrease the likelihood that the behavior will happen again. Consequences teach. Whether intentional or not, every consequence sends a message. Positive reinforcement can encourage desired behaviors, while unintentional positive reinforcement (like laughing out loud at an undesirable behavior) can accidentally maintain or worsen challenging behaviors. Pay close attention and be intentional in your reactions and responses to behaviors. They can make or break you.

Examples:

- Gaining attention from an adult or peer
- Receiving praise or a reward
- Being removed from a task
- Losing a privilege

Tips for Using the ABC Log:

- **Be specific and objective**: Avoid vague terms like "acted out." Describe precisely what you observed.
- **Track Patterns**: Look for repeated antecedents or consequences that may be reinforcing unwanted behaviors.
- **Reflect regularly**: Write and use anecdotal notes to consider what changes might be needed in the environment or routine.
- **Collaborate**: Share behavioral and anecdotal logs with parents, counselors, or support staff to work as a team.

Dr. Gwen's Tip, Tool, or Strategy:

ABC Behavior Log Sample

Date/Time	Antecedent (What happened right before?)	Behavior (What the child did)	Consequence (What happened after?)	Reflection
9/15 8:30 AM	The teacher asked students to begin independent reading.	The student put their head down and said, "I'm not doing this!"	The teacher allowed the student to sit quietly while checking in with other students.	Possible work avoidance: The student may be feeling overwhelmed or incompetent
9/16 10:15 AM	Transitioning from class to art was announced	The student ran ahead, ignoring the teacher's request to line up.	The student was asked to return and go to the end of the line	May need more explicit transition cues or visual reminders.
9/16 2:00 PM	Group assignment required working with a peer.	The student yelled, "I'm not working with him!" and walked out of the room.	The student was reassigned to a solo task.	The student may need support with social skills and conflict resolution.

B

One kind word

can change

someone's entire day.

~ Unknown

B – Behavior Charts

Behavior charts are widely used tools in homes, classrooms, and counseling settings to encourage positive behavior and help children track their progress. When used correctly, behavior charts can empower children, build responsibility, and reinforce desired behaviors in a motivating and structured way, helping children stay focused on their goals.

A behavior chart is a visual tool that can be used individually or for groups to track specific behaviors and progress over time. When used consistently and positively, behavior charts provide immediate feedback, making expectations clear and progress visible. This clarity can boost motivation, build self-esteem, and foster a sense of accomplishment as children see their efforts yield rewards or recognition. Behavior charts also encourage accountability and responsibility, helping children track their own choices and reflect on their actions. For adults, charts offer a consistent tool to monitor behavior patterns, celebrate improvements, and guide supportive conversations with children.

Behavior charts can take many forms, but the core purpose remains the same: to support, motivate, and reinforce behavioral goals.

Types of Behavior Charts

1. **Daily Behavior Charts**: Focus on 1-2 target behaviors (e.g., follow directions, complete assigned tasks). Points or stickers are awarded throughout the day.

2. **Weekly Goal Charts**: Help track progress toward broader goals over an extended period (e.g., no physical aggression — hitting, kicking, throwing, or biting).

3. **Color System Charts**: Children move their clip/card up or down based on their behavior (e.g., green = great day, yellow = 1-2 warnings, red = 3 or more warnings)

4. **Token Economy Charts**: Children earn tokens or points for exhibiting positive behavior, which they can exchange for rewards (e.g., free time, prize box, or privileges).

5. **Personalized Self-Monitoring Charts**: Older children track their own behaviors and reflect at the end of the day or week. Self-monitoring builds ownership and insight.

Steps to Create an Effective Behavior Chart

1. **Choose the Target Behavior(s)**: Be clear and specific (e.g., raise your hand before speaking instead of 'be good').

2. **Make It Visual and Age-Appropriate**: Use visuals for younger children; use checkboxes or reflection spaces for older ones.

3. **Define the Reward System**: Will the child earn a daily prize, weekly incentive, or points to trade for prizes.

4. **Be Consistent**: Use the chart every day at the same time and in the same way. Inconsistency leads to confusion of expectations and decreases effectiveness.

5. **Celebrate Small Wins**: Focus on effort and progress, not perfection. Offer praise and encouragement, even if the chart isn't complete.

Dr. Gwen's Tip, Tool, or Strategy:

While behavior charts can be effective for some children, they may not work for everyone, especially when used without a supportive and understanding approach. Charts that focus solely on compliance or punishment can cause shame, frustration, or a sense of failure in children who struggle to meet expectations due to underlying challenges like Attention Deficit Hyperactivity Disorder (ADHD), autism, trauma, or emotional dysregulation. If the chart is too rigid, lacks consistency, or fails to address the root causes of behavior, it may lose its impact or even backfire, resulting in regression rather than progression. Children may also become overly focused on external rewards, rather than developing internal motivation or self-regulation skills. For behavior charts to be successful, they must be paired with empathy, realistic goals, and ongoing support that honors the child's individual needs.

When used with care, compassion, and consistency, behavior charts can help children develop accountability, foster emotional awareness, and work toward behavioral transformation. They are a positive, practical, and personalized step on the journey from chaos to calm.

Common Mistakes to Avoid

- **Too many goals at once**: Having too many goals can overwhelm children and be cumbersome to manage. Start with 1 to 2 behaviors.
- **Inconsistent use**: Charts lose meaning if they are not used daily or reviewed with the child.
- **Lack of clarity**: Ensure the child understands what each behavior looks like when performed correctly and how to achieve success. For example, having too many colors on a color system chart with unclear rules and expectations is ineffective. Please keep it simple. Far too often, when consulting with parents, neither they nor the child can explain the classroom behavior charts regarding the difference between being orange and purple. Let me say that eight colors for a classroom behavior chart is too many, regardless of the grade, but especially for kindergarten and first grade. Stop it, it's too much!
- **No follow-up or fading plan**: Behavior charts are tools, not permanent solutions. Plan to slowly reduce use as behaviors improve.

C

The way we

talk

to our children

becomes

their inner

voice.

~ Peggy O'Mara

C – Communication and Expectations

Before behavior can change, children must understand what is expected of them and feel safe, supported, and respected. Clear communication and consistent expectations are the cornerstones of positive behavior support. Without them, even the best strategies will fall short. Let us explore how intentional communication and clearly defined expectations reduce chaos, increase trust, and support long-term behavior growth.

Why Communication Matters

Children don't always misbehave to be difficult. Often, they:

- Don't understand what's expected.
- Feel overwhelmed or anxious.
- Are testing boundaries in search of safety or consistency.
- Lack the skills to respond appropriately.

Communication and expectations are like the GPS of behavior transformation. When adults are clear about the destination, consistent with their directions, and flexible when children take a wrong turn, we guide them not only toward better behavior but also toward growth, confidence, and connection.

Expectations are the rules and routines that set the tone for how we interact with one another, resolve conflicts, and manage challenges.

Children thrive on predictability. When adults speak with clarity, empathy, and purpose, children are more likely to feel secure, seen, and ready to cooperate. When expectations are consistent, they feel more secure and less likely to act out.

Dr. Gwen's Tip, Tool, or Strategy:

- Children may feel confused or test boundaries.
- Never assume a child knows what to do. Teach explicitly.
- Celebrate small wins and effort, not just achieved goals.
- Model calm, assertive communication even when frustrated.
- Clear, concise, and consistent communication and expectations help you reach your goal.
- Display clear, age-appropriate rules and review them often.
- Use communication logs to share information about behaviors and strategies between home and school for consistency.
- Provide behavior-specific feedback by sharing detailed comments, such as "I love how you shared your toys," instead of just saying, "Good Job."
- Utilize flexible expectations to adjust expectations based on individual needs and developmental stages.

D

Play
is the highest
form of
research.

~ Albert Einstein

D — Data Tracking — Making Behavior Visible

To move from chaos to calm in a child's behavior, we must do more than observe; we must **track**. Data tracking provides us with insight, reveals patterns, and supports informed decision-making. Whether you are a parent, teacher, counselor, or caregiver, tracking behavior over time helps you respond more effectively rather than simply react.

When we collect meaningful data, we shift from guessing to understanding, from frustration to strategy, and from overwhelm to empowerment. Tracking behavior is critical because it helps parents, teachers, and caregivers understand patterns, triggers, and progress over time. Rather than relying on memory or emotion in the moment, tracking provides precise data that can inform more effective decisions and interventions, as well as support documentation for IEPs, 504 plans, and counseling referrals. It allows adults to identify what's working, what needs to change, and when certain behaviors are more likely to occur. This insight makes it easier to adjust strategies, reinforce positive behavior, and address challenges with consistency and intention. Over time, tracking helps shift the focus from reacting to behavior to proactively supporting long-term growth and self-regulation.

You don't need to be a behavior specialist to use data; you just need to be consistent and intentional in your approach. Here are some simple formats:

Types of Data to Track

1. Frequency

Definition: How often a behavior occurs

Use for: Tracking repeated behaviors (e.g., how many times a student calls out in class).

Date	Behavior	Frequency	Notes
8/15	Talking out of turn	1111 4 Times	Reading group (15-minute span of time)

2. Duration

Definition: How long the behavior lasts.

Use for: Behaviors such as tantrums, off-task time, or screen use.

Date	Behavior	Duration	Notes
8/16	Tantrum (crying, screaming)	8:20 - 8:40 a.m. 20 Minutes	Started when it was time to transition from free time to Math

3. Latency

Definition: The time it takes to begin a behavior after a prompt or instruction.

Use for: Behaviors related to compliance, transitioning, or responsiveness.

Date	Prompt	Behavior begins after	Notes
8/17	The teacher says to start working.	10:00 – 10:08 a.m. 8 Minutes	Daydreaming or distracted

4. Magnitude

Definition: The intensity or severity of a behavior.

Use for: Behaviors that can vary in strength or disruption level (e.g., tantrums, aggression, voice volume).

When tracking magnitude in behavior data, using a scale provides a structured way to capture the intensity or severity of a behavior beyond simply noting whether it happened. Magnitude reflects the strength, disruptiveness, or impact of a behavior, which is particularly useful for behaviors that vary in force, duration, or emotional expression. Using a numeric or descriptive scale helps quantify this intensity in a consistent and meaningful way.

For example:

Sample Magnitude Scale:

- **1 – Mild** (e.g., quiet refusal, eye roll, low-volume whining)
- **2 – Moderate** (e.g., verbal outburst, walking away, slamming a door)
- **3 – Severe** (e.g., yelling, throwing objects, hitting)

This type of scale helps teachers, parents, or therapists:

Date	Behavior	Magnitude	Description
8/18	Tantrum 1:15 p.m.	3	Screaming, stomping, and throwing objects
8/19	Tantrum 2:30 p.m.	1	Whining and light crying, no aggression

5. Rate

Definition: The frequency of the behavior divided by time (behavior per minute/hour/day).

Use for: Standardizing behavior across different lengths of observation.

Example: A counselor observes a child for 30 minutes and notes 12 instances of leaving their seat.

Date	Behavior	Total Events	Observation Time	Rate
8/20	Left the seat without permission	12	30 minutes	0.4 minute

6. Goal Progress

Definition: Tracks steps toward a behavior goal

Use for: Self-regulation, social skills, or routines.

Week	Goal	Achieved	Notes
1	Engage with a peer during play 2X per week	✓	Self-initiated once

Dr. Gwen's Tip, Tool, or Strategy:

Tracking behavior doesn't have to be tedious. It's a bridge between what we observe and how we can help. When we take time to gather consistent data, we gain clarity, reduce frustration, and design smarter, more compassionate responses that truly transform behavior from chaos to calm.

Select the type of tracking that fits the behavior and your capacity to record it with consistency and fidelity. Even small data sets can offer powerful insights when paired with reflection.

27

E

When little people
are overwhelmed
by big emotions,
it's our job
to share our calm,
not join their chaos.

~ L.R. Knost

E — Emotional Regulation

Imagine expecting a child to solve a math problem while they're in the middle of a meltdown. Consider asking them to express their feelings when they're too overwhelmed to speak. Adults often have unrealistic expectations. For example, instead of modeling how to take deep breaths during a meltdown, we ask kids to tell us what's wrong. Emotional regulation is the ability to recognize, express, and manage emotions appropriately. It is at the heart of all behavior. Without it, calm can't be obtained or sustained. With it, transformation becomes possible.

In this section, we will explore what emotional regulation entails, why some children struggle with it, and how to help them label and understand their emotions. We will also discuss how adults can model and teach children coping skills using compassion, empathy, and intention.

Why Emotional Regulation Is Hard for Some Kids

Some children haven't learned these skills yet, especially if they:

- have experienced trauma or chronic stress.
- struggle with sensory processing or neurodivergence.
- have limited language or coping tools.
- live in unpredictable environments.
- see dysregulation modeled by adults.

For these children, big feelings = big reactions. Our role as caregivers is not to suppress emotions but to support emotional literacy and teach effective regulation strategies. When we teach kids how to ride the emotional waves instead of drowning in them, we give them a lifelong skill that supports better relationships, stronger learning, and real confidence.

Practical Strategies for Teaching Emotional Regulation

1. Name the Emotion

Use visuals, such as books or charts, like the Mood Meter or Zones of Regulation, to help children develop vocabulary for expressing their feelings.

2. Use Calm-Down Tools

Create a toolbox of regulation options such as:

- Practice deep breathing (e.g., "smell the flower, blow out the candle")
- Use stress balls or fidgets
- Use sensory Items (e.g., stuffed animals, weighted blankets)
- Take movement breaks
- Draw or journal to express your feelings
- Put together a puzzle
- Listen to soothing music
- Take a short walk or stretch
- Splash water on your face
- Hold an ice cube or rub a cool cloth
- Use a calm-down corner or safe space

3. Teach Coping Skills Outside the Moment

Don't teach during a meltdown; teach during calm times. Role-play, read stories, or create "What helps me when I'm upset" lists. Use collaborative problem solving with children to brainstorm solutions when issues arise or after a calm-down period.

For example, I once had a student, after a 30-minute tantrum, ask, "Why didn't you turn on some music?"

4. Build Routine and Predictability

Transitions and surprises can spike anxiety. Prepare kids in advance and give them choices when possible.

For example:

Would you like to take your noise-canceling headphones to lunch?

Do you want to go to the assembly or stay in Ms. Brown's room?

5. Model Regulation Yourself

Let children hear you say:

- "I feel frustrated, so I'm taking deep breaths."
- "This is hard, but I'm trying to stay calm. I know I can do this."
- "I'm getting frustrated, let me take a break and come back to this in a few minutes."

Children learn from what we do and what we say.

Red Flags That May Need Additional Support

- Regular meltdowns that last more than 30 minutes
- Verbal or physical aggression that does not respond to calming strategies
- Inability to name or talk about feelings, even with support
- Signs of anxiety or depression

In such instances, consider consulting a school counselor, behavioral specialist, or child therapist for guidance and support.

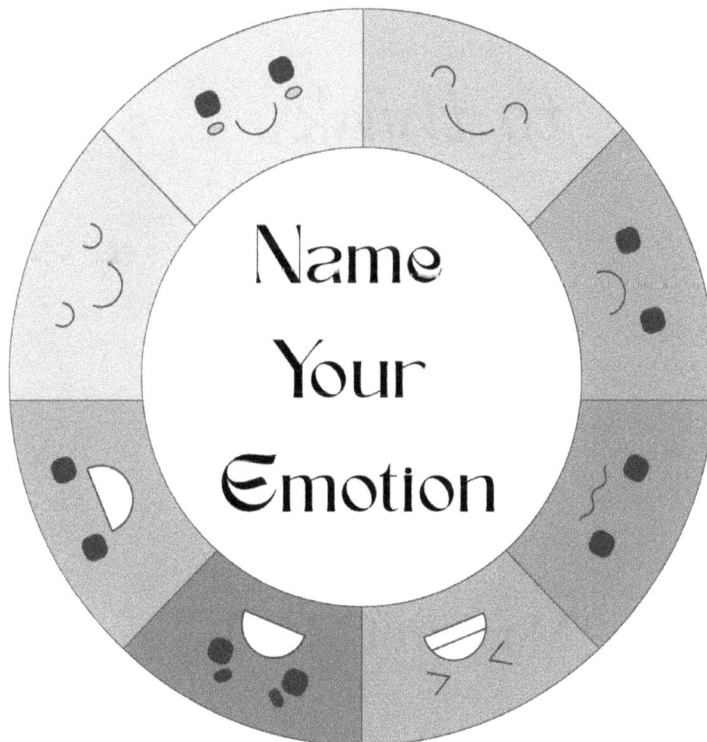

Name Your Emotion

F

Children must be

taught how

to think,

not what

to think.

~ Margaret Mead

F — Functions of Behavior

Children don't just "act out" for no reason. Every behavior has a purpose, especially the ones that frustrate us most. Whether a child is throwing a tantrum, constantly interrupting, or refusing to follow directions, their behavior is trying to communicate a need.

Understanding the function (intention or need) behind a behavior helps us respond more effectively and compassionately. Rather than simply reacting, we can strategize to meet the underlying need behind the behavior while teaching more effective ways to express it.

When we treat only the behavior without understanding the function, we miss the chance to teach and support more effective behaviors. But when we align our response to the why, we empower children to:

- Learn appropriate ways to meet their needs
- Trust the adults around them
- Reduce the frequency of challenging behaviors over time

What Are the Functions of Behavior?

In behavioral science, there are five primary reasons (functions) why a child may engage in challenging or disruptive behaviors. Using the T.E.A.M.S. framework helps parents, teachers, and caregivers better understand the reasons behind a child's behavior.

By identifying whether behavior is driven by a need for Tangible items, Escape or avoidance, Attention, Medical concerns, or Sensory input, adults can respond with empathy and intention rather than frustration or punishment. Recognizing the true function of a behavior enables more effective and compassionate interventions that address the child's underlying needs. Instead of focusing solely on stopping the behavior, the T.E.A.M.S. approach encourages us to ask, "What is this behavior trying to communicate?" and respond in a way that promotes growth, connection, and long-term behavior transformation. Beyond just the acronym, T.E.A.M.S. is also a reminder that supporting a child's behavioral growth requires a team approach, with caregivers, educators, counselors, and other professionals working together across home and school settings. Collaboration, consistency, and communication among all members of the child's support team are essential in helping them move from chaos to calm.

1. Tangibles or Activities

Goal: To get something the child wants, an object, snack, toy, device, or a preferred activity.

What it looks like:

- Crying or yelling for a toy
- Demanding snacks or electronics
- Refusing to give up a preferred activity

Examples:

A child throws a tantrum in the store to get a toy.

A student rushes through work to get to computer time.

Support Strategies:

- Set clear expectations and boundaries around rewards.
- Use visual schedules or first/then prompts, such as "First homework, then iPad."
- Reinforce asking appropriately and following directions.
- Reward appropriate asking and waiting.

2. Escape or Avoidance

Goal: To get out of or away from an activity, demand, or environment the child finds complicated, boring, overwhelming, or unpleasant.

What it looks like:

- Running away or hiding.
- Saying "I don't know" or "I can't".
- Complaining or becoming disruptive before or during a nonpreferred task.

Examples:

A student acts out when asked to read independently.

A child fakes illness to avoid going to school.

Support Strategies:

- Modify the task to be more manageable (shorten, simplify, or give support).
- Provide breaks and use tools like "help" cards.
- Offer choices and breaks.
- Gradually build tolerance for non-preferred activities.
- Build coping skills for stressful situations.

3. Attention

Goal: To get noticed, gain interaction, or feel connected, even if the attention is negative.

What It Looks Like:

- Talking out of turn
- Making jokes or silly noises
- Interrupting conversations
- Acting out when you're busy

Examples:

A student makes jokes in class to get peers to laugh.

A child whines, yells, or constantly interrupts when a parent is on the phone.

Support Strategies:

- Offer positive attention before the behavior occurs ("I love how you're playing quietly!").
- Teach appropriate ways to get attention (e.g., raising a hand, using polite words).
- Ignore minor attention-seeking behaviors when safe to do so.
- Provide regular check-ins or praise.

4. Medical

Purpose: To relieve discomfort, cope with pain, or react to physiological distress that the child may not be able to explain or understand.

Medical is considered a function of behavior when a child's actions are primarily a response to internal physical discomfort, illness, or undiagnosed medical conditions, rather than a desire for attention, escape, access, or sensory input.

What It Looks Like:
- Unexplained aggression or irritability
- Fatigue or excessive sleepiness
- Withdrawal or refusal to participate
- Repetitive self-injurious behavior (e.g., hitting oneself, headbanging)
- Sudden regression in previously mastered behaviors or skills
- Avoidance of food, physical activity, or light
- Complaints of pain or discomfort

Examples:
A student who was once social becomes withdrawn and self-isolates.
A student refuses to eat lunch or lashes out after recess.
A student begins hitting their head on the desk during math lessons.

Support Strategies:
- Document behavior patterns to identify connections to specific times of day, food, or activity.
- Communicate with caregivers about health, history, recent illness, or ongoing medical concerns.
- Refer to medical professionals (pediatrician, neurologist, allergist, etc. for evaluation.)

5. Sensory or Automatic Reinforcement

Goal: To feel good or relieve discomfort. The behavior meets a physical or internal need.

What It Looks Like:

- Rocking, spinning, hand-flipping
- Humming, chewing on objects • Repetitive movements or noises

Examples:

A child rocks back and forth for comfort.

A student taps a pencil rhythmically or chews on clothes.

Support Strategies:

- Offer sensory alternatives (fidgets, chewable jewelry, calming tools).
- Build sensory breaks into the day.
- Consult with occupational therapists for specific sensory needs.
- Adjust your expectations and provide temporary flexibility during a flare-up.
- Use sensory accommodation to reduce physical discomfort (e.g., dim lights, quiet spaces).
- Avoid punishment for behaviors that may be pain-related or uncomfortable.

Intervening with typical behavior strategies alone (e.g., consequences or behavior charts) won't address the root cause if the behavior is medically driven. Instead, it may increase the child's distress and reinforce misunderstandings.

You should always consider and rule out medical causes when there's a sudden change in behavior, especially in children with limited verbal communication. Medical behaviors may be misinterpreted as defiance or disobedience.

How to Identify the Function of a Behavior

Ask yourself:

1. What happened **before** the behavior (antecedent)?
2. What happened immediately **after** the behavior (consequence)?
3. Does the behavior help the child **obtain** something or **avoid** something?

Remember, as we discussed in A, using an ABC chart (Antecedent–Behavior–Consequence) can help track patterns and identify the why (function) of behavior over time. When we take the time to decode the "why," we don't just change behavior; we build trust, connection, and a better path forward. Behavior is communication. Our job is to listen with curiosity, not judgment.

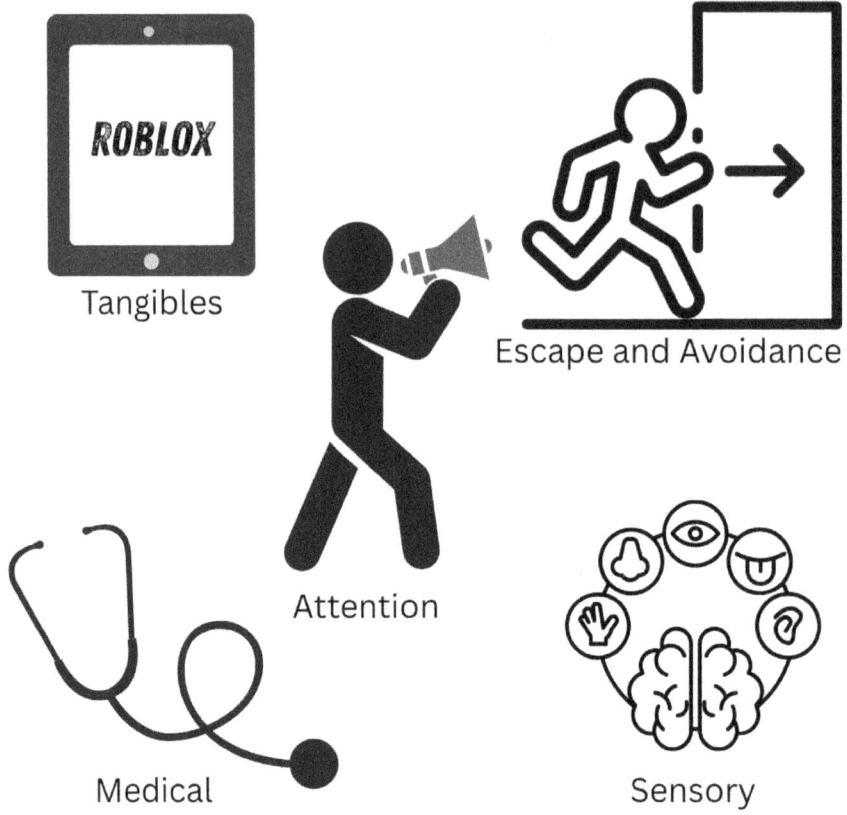

Tangibles

Attention

Escape and Avoidance

Medical

Sensory

T.E.A.M.S

G

Be the adult
you needed
when you
were a child.

~ Unknown

G – Goal Setting

Goals are essential because they provide direction, purpose, and a sense of accomplishment. When children set goals, they learn how to focus their efforts, stay motivated, and work through challenges. Goal setting develops critical life skills, including responsibility, perseverance, and decision-making. It also fosters a growth mindset by helping children understand that progress often comes from effort and learning from mistakes. Achieving a goal, big or small, boosts confidence and encourages children to keep striving for personal and academic success. Overall, goal setting helps children develop self-awareness and empowers them to take ownership of their actions and future.

Teach children to set **SMART** goals:

- Specific – Clear and understandable
- Measurable – Track progress and results
- Achievable – Realistic for their age and ability
- Relevant – Important to the child's needs
- Time-bound – Set with a deadline or timeframe

Types of Goals Children Can Set

Categories	Examples
Academic	I will read three books this month to improve my reading skills.
Behavioral	I will raise my hand instead of shouting out to earn a trip to the treasure box.
Emotional	I will practice calming breaths when I get upset so I won't get in trouble.
Social	I will share during group time to make more friends.
Personal Growth	I will try something new at recess to learn a new skill.

One of my most memorable examples of the power of goal setting is helping students prepare for standardized testing. By educating parents and students on how to read score reports and helping them chart their scores and set realistic improvement goals, we saw tremendous improvement across content areas and grade levels. I distinctly remember a sixth-grade student, whom I will name John, who was shocked by his test scores in comparison to his peers, when we analyzed the data as a class. John argued that he was smarter than all of the kids in his class. We had an ongoing debate about the validity of his test scores. I challenged John to prove how smart he truly was on the upcoming tests. This debate ignited a fire within John as he had something to prove. I must admit that I was a little skeptical of the goals John set for himself in each content area, and we discussed how realistic his goals were to attain. I'm happy to say that when scores came back the following year, John proved to be not only the smartest in his class but also across the board for his grade level in all academic areas, except for one area where a classmate, if I'm remembering correctly, either matched his score or scored one point higher. John proved that some kids only need a little motivation to achieve their goals. I wonder where John is now, as he had aspired to attend the Massachusetts Institute of Technology (MIT).

Dr. Gwen's Tip, Tool, or Strategy:

Here are some goal-tracking tips you may find helpful.
1. Behavior Contracts: Use behavior contracts to collaboratively set goals and consequences with your child, encouraging accountability.

2. Token Economy System: Reward positive behaviors with tokens (stickers, points) that can be exchanged for rewards, such as extra playtime.

3. Check-In/Check-Out System: Meet with students at the start and end of the day to review goals and progress. This usually occurs with identified students and is often implemented in the Response To Intervention (RTI) process. It's also often used by school counselors to support students.

Additional goal-tracking tools you may find helpful.

1. Sticker charts
2. Weekly goal-setting journals
3. Color-coded calendars
4. Bulletin board displays
5. Classroom goal posters

What you're supposed to do when you don't like a thing is change it. If you can't change it, change the way you think about it. Don't complain.

– Maya Angelou

H

See the light
in others,
and treat them
as if that is
all you see.

~ Wayne Dyer

H – Hobbies & Interests

Encouraging hobbies and exploring interests in children provides numerous developmental benefits that extend far beyond leisure and pastimes. When children engage in activities they enjoy, hobbies and interests become vital outlets for self-expression, creativity, emotional regulation, and skill development. Engaging in enjoyable activities can help develop passions and persistence, serve as a buffer against stress, enhance children's sense of identity, and provide a positive outlet for energy and emotions. These experiences foster self-esteem as children gain confidence in their abilities and feel a sense of accomplishment. Social hobbies also help form healthy relationships by building communication and teamwork skills, while solitary hobbies can promote focus and independence. Exploring a variety of interests allows children to discover what excites and motivates them, encouraging a healthy sense of curiosity and a growth or "try-it" mindset, and discover their unique talents, passions, and purpose. By observing the activities that capture a child's attention and energy, adults can help nurture their natural talents and support their growth into well-rounded, resilient individuals.

Here are a few reflection prompts for children.

1. What do you love doing when no one tells you what to do?
2. What makes you feel calm or happy?
3. What's something you've always wanted to try?

Types of Hobbies and Interests

Encourage them. They will get better with practice.

Category	Examples
Creative	Drawing, painting, storytelling, theater, crafting
Physical	Dance, cheer, sports, biking, swimming, yoga
Academic	Reading, science kits, math games, coding, STEM
Musical	Playing an instrument, singing, rhythm games
Nature-Based	Gardening, hiking, collecting rocks/insects
Building and Tinkering	LEGO, puzzles, building model kits, fixing things
Social	Volunteering, clubs, board games, the debate team
Mindful/Quiet	Journaling, knitting, origami, meditation

How Adults Can Support

- Provide materials and time to explore different activities.
- Observe and listen to what excites or soothes your child.
- Avoid pressure on performance. Focus on fun, not perfection.
- Celebrate progress, not just outcomes.
- Model hobby exploration by sharing your interests.

I

No act of kindness,
no matter how small,
is ever wasted.

~ Aesop

1 – Incentives/Rewards

Children thrive on encouragement and recognition. Incentives and rewards are powerful tools that can reinforce positive behavior and emotional growth, support the formation of new habits, and increase motivation for children to engage in desired behaviors, especially when trying something new or overcoming a challenge.

Benefits of Incentives and Rewards:
- Reinforce effort and progress, not just outcomes.
- Help build self-confidence and teach the value of perseverance.
- Clarify expectations and provide a clear understanding of which behaviors are appreciated
- Create opportunities for connection and encouragement between children and adults
- Promote a sense of achievement and motivation to keep going

When used appropriately, rewards and incentives teach children that their actions lead to meaningful outcomes. They also foster a sense of pride and ownership in the choices they make.

Please be advised that incentives should not be used to bribe children. Incentives should be part of a structured support system. They help children see the value in trying, improving, and staying consistent.

Types of Incentives and Rewards

Type	Examples
Tangible	Stickers, tokens, certificates, small prizes, coupons, healthy snacks
Social	Praise, high-fives, fist pumps, phone calls home, class shoutouts, inviting a friend to a special activity, lunch with the teacher.
Activity	Extra playtime, special helper roles, games
Privileges	Screen time: select dinner or a movie, stay up 30 minutes later, sit in a special seat, choose the next book or activity.
Creative	Positive notes, reward jars, spin-the-wheel reward chart, mystery bag

Note: Incentives should always be age-appropriate and aligned with the child's interests.

Dr. Gwen's Tip, Tool, or Strategy:

Guidelines for Effective Use

- Be Clear and Consistent: Clearly explain the behavior you're encouraging and the reward that follows.
- Keep It Proportional: Match the effort to the reward, small wins deserve small celebrations, big milestones deserve more.
- Use as Teaching Tools: Tie rewards to values like kindness, perseverance, or following directions.
- Focus on Effort Over Outcome: Reward the process of trying and improving rather than perfection.
- Fade Over Time: As new behaviors become habits, gradually reduce tangible rewards and replace them with internal motivators.
- Use conversations, reflection, and emotional praise to help children recognize how their positive actions benefit themselves and others.

J

Journaling increases your self-confidence. It helps you look at how far you've come and how you overcame previous seemingly impossible obstacles.

~ Jeremiah Say

J – Journal (Gratitude, Reflection, Mood, Drawing).

Journaling is a simple yet powerful tool that supports children's emotional growth, self-awareness, and behavior transformation. It provides a safe space to express their thoughts, feelings, and experiences, which helps reduce being emotionally-overwhelm and encourages healthy self-reflection. Through regular journaling and reflection, children begin to develop self-awareness, recognizing patterns in their emotions and behaviors. This reflection can lead to better decision-making and problem-solving skills. Journaling also supports literacy and communication by strengthening writing abilities and encouraging the use of expressive language. It helps children put words to what they are experiencing, which reduces emotional overload and improves communication skills.

Additionally, journaling fosters mindfulness by allowing children to slow down, focus on the present moment, and reflect on their day with intention. Over time, journaling helps children build resilience, celebrate progress, and take ownership of their personal growth. Whether through words, drawings, or creative prompts, journaling becomes a quiet conversation with the self. It's a place where feelings can be named, thoughts organized, and behaviors understood.

Dr. Gwen's Tip, Tool, Strategy:

Here are themed journal prompts for children that encourage self-reflection, emotional growth, and creative thinking. You can use these in a guided journal, such as the **D.E.A.R. Journal (Drop Everything and Reflect)**, which can also be used as a daily or weekly writing activity.

Themes

Self-Awareness

What makes me feel happy?

One thing I'm really good at is...

A time I felt proud of myself was when...

When I feel upset, I usually...

Kindness & Relationships

What does being a good friend mean to me?

A time I helped someone and how it felt:

Someone I admire and why:

What can I do to make someone smile today?

Courage & Confidence

Something I tried even though I was scared:

A time I didn't give up was when...

I feel brave when I...

One way I can believe in myself more is...

Emotional Regulation

When I get angry, I can try to...

Three things that help me calm down are:

What do my body and mind feel like when I'm nervous?

Draw your "calm place" — real or imaginary.

Goal Setting & Growth

A goal I want to reach this month:

What steps can I take to reach my goal?

Something I'm working hard to improve is...

What would my best future self look and feel like?

Gratitude & Positivity

Three things I'm thankful for today:

One person who makes my life better:

Something small that brought me joy today:

Draw or list your "happiness toolbox."

Creativity & Imagination

If I could invent anything, it would be...

Write a story about a superhero version of you.

What would your dream day look like?

Design your perfect classroom, home, or world!

K

They may forget

what you said,

but they will never

forget how

you made them feel.

~ Maya Angelou

K – Key phrases

Children learn not only by what we say, but also by **how** we say it and **how often** we say it. In moments of chaos or calm, the words adults choose become powerful tools for shaping emotional responses and guiding behavior. This section examines the significance of employing clear, consistent, and compassionate language to foster, redirect, and reinforce positive behaviors at home and in school. When parents, teachers, and caregivers use shared language cues, children experience a sense of safety, predictability, and trust. Whether it's a gentle reminder to "try that again the calm way" or a validating phrase like "you're the boss of your body," these intentional but straightforward phrases create a bridge between emotional support and behavior change. In this section, you'll find practical examples, reflection tools, and ready-to-use phrases that can transform challenging moments into teachable ones, moving children from chaos to calm with words rooted in connection.

Key phrases can be used to prompt desired behavior. Here is where intentional language comes in. Key phrases are designed to help parents, teachers, counselors, and caregivers use calm, purposeful communication that supports behavioral growth. These consistent language cues not only guide children toward positive behavior but also build emotional safety and trust. Especially, when used across various environments, including at home, in school, and in the community, these phrases create a shared language that reinforces expectations, reduces power struggles, and promotes meaningful transformation. Just as the T.E.A.M.S. framework reminds us that it takes a collaborative approach to support a child's needs, these phrases serve as everyday tools that align the entire team in helping children move from chaos to calm.

Here are some practical, easy-to-use phrases that can be integrated into everyday interactions to prompt and reinforce the behaviors you want to see, creating consistency, connection, and calm across settings.

Transition & Routine Support

- "First this, then that." (e.g., "First clean up, then snack.")
- "Let's try that again, the calm way."
- "It's time to switch. What's your next step?"
- "You're not in trouble. I want to help you."
- "Let's take a break and come back stronger."

Clear Expectations

- "I'm looking for safe hands, safe feet, and kind words."
- "Show me what being ready looks like."
- "Use your inside voice so everyone can feel calm."
- "Hands are for helping, not hurting. Hitting hurts our bodies and our feelings."
- "It's okay if you don't like it or agree, but you do have to be respectful."

Emotional Regulation & Reflection

- "Let's pause and breathe together."
- "How is your body feeling right now?"
- "Let's name that feeling so we can tame it."
- "You can be mad, but you can't be mean. It's not okay to hurt others' bodies or feelings."

Promoting Self-Control, Accountability & Ownership

- "You're the boss of your body. You can choose not to hit."
- "What can you do to fix this?"
- "You can make a different choice."
- "Let's rewind or reverse, and try again."
- "How can we solve this together?"

Encouragement & Positive Reinforcement

- "I noticed you kept trying. That shows perseverance and resilience!"
- "Thank you for using your words. That was powerful."
- "You made a respectful choice. I'm proud of you."
- "That was a big feeling, and you handled it with courage."
- "Look at you staying calm, making good choices, and being mature."

Empathy & Connection

- I'm here to help you. You can do hard things."
- "You're not alone. We can figure this out together."
- "You matter, and your feelings matter too."
- "This is a tough moment; your behavior was not great, but you are a great kid."
- "Let's find a way through this, side by side."

Dr. Gwen's Tip, Tool, or Strategy:

From Chaos to Calm

- Chaos is loud, but calm is powerful.
- Transformation starts with a pause.
- Before we can change behavior, we must calm the storm.
- You can't teach calm if you aren't calm.

Connection Before Correction

- Connect first, correct second.
- Safe relationships create safe behavior.
- Regulation before redirection.
- Empathy opens the door to change.

L

I've learned

that I still have

a lot to learn.

~ Maya Angelou

L – Learned helplessness

Sometimes the biggest obstacle to change isn't a child's behavior, it's a child's belief that they can't change. Learned helplessness occurs when children, after repeated struggles or failed attempts, begin to believe that their actions no longer matter. Learned helplessness may manifest as resistance, passivity, or even defiance, but beneath the surface lies a child who has lost faith in their ability to succeed. This mindset can lead to withdrawal, lack of effort, or overdependence on adults, even in tasks they are capable of doing. In the context of behavior transformation, addressing learned helplessness is essential. If left unchallenged, it reinforces low self-esteem and shuts down growth opportunities. This section explores what learned helplessness looks like in children, its origins, and how parents and educators can gently reframe it through supportive language, scaffolded success, and belief-building strategies.

I've observed how parents and teachers fail to watch children struggle, especially when the task seems overwhelming or when emotions run high. Out of love, concern, or a desire to keep things moving smoothly, adults may step in and do things for children rather than guiding them to do it themselves. Sometimes this is done to save time in a busy day or to avoid a meltdown or power struggle. While these intentions come from a caring place, consistently stepping in can unintentionally send the message that the child isn't capable, reinforcing patterns of learned helplessness.

Over time, children may stop trying altogether, relying on adults to rescue them instead of building the confidence and skills they need to persevere through challenges.

Demonstrating belief in children's capabilities, shown through consistent encouragement and opportunities for meaningful effort, can be the spark that moves them from powerless to empowered. Our goal is to help every child rediscover their voice, effort, and confidence, moving them from "I give up" to "I can try again." With the proper support, patience, and opportunities to experience small successes, children can unlearn helplessness and begin to rebuild a sense of capability and hope. The path from "I can't" to "I did it!" is paved with patience, structure, and trust.

Signs of Learned Helplessness in Children

- Avoids tasks without trying
- Shuts down when faced with mild difficulty
- Becomes overly dependent on adult help
- Rarely takes initiative
- Low frustration tolerance
- Uses defeatist language: "I'm just dumb.," "I can't do it.," "It's too hard."
- Reluctant to make decisions

Strategies to Transform Helplessness Into Hope

1. **Scaffold success:** Break tasks into manageable steps so children experience small wins that rebuild confidence.

2. **Praise effort, not outcome:** Shift focus from results to persistence: "I saw you kept trying even when it got tricky, that's brave."

3. **Use growth-mindset language:** Model and repeat phrases like:

   "Mistakes help us learn."

   "You haven't mastered it YET."

   "What could you try differently next time?"

4. **Provide limited choices:** Empower children by offering them a choice between two acceptable options. Choice initiates action.

5. **Create "stretch zones":** Gently push children out of their comfort zone with support. Too much challenge = panic; too little = boredom.

6. **Stop rescuing them too quickly:** Let them struggle, productively. Offer encouragement, not solutions.

7. **Use reflective questioning:**

   "What part of this do you know how to do?"

   "What's one thing you can try first?"

   "What helped last time?"

Rebuilding Trust in Themselves

Children who have experienced learned helplessness need consistent caregivers who believe in their potential, even when they may not believe in themselves yet. Transforming helplessness begins not with high expectations, but with high empathy. It's about holding space for their fear while holding them accountable to keep trying.

Behavior Cue Phrases for Parents & Teachers

"Let's figure it out together. What's your first step?"

"I'll stay close while you try."

"I won't do it for you, I know you can do hard things."

"You've done hard things before, remember when you ___?"

"Put forth your best effort, even if it doesn't go perfectly."

yes you can

M

Your children
will become
who you are,
so be who
you want
them to be.

~ unknown

M – Modeling

Children are always watching and learning. Whether we realize it or not, they take cues from the adults around them to understand how to behave, express emotions, solve problems, and interact with others. Modeling is one of the most powerful (and often overlooked) tools for behavior transformation. In this section, we examine how adult behaviors influence children's behaviors, both positively and negatively, and how intentional modeling can help children develop emotional regulation, empathy, responsibility, and respect. To help children move from chaos to calm, we must first look in the mirror and model the calm we want them to see and emulate.

Modeling matters because children learn more from what they observe than from what they are told. When adults consistently demonstrate calm, respectful, and thoughtful behavior, children begin to internalize these actions as the norm. Whether it's managing frustration, solving problems, or showing kindness, children watch how the adults in their lives handle situations and often copy them. Modeling provides a powerful, nonverbal message about how to navigate the world and build healthy relationships. When parents, teachers, and caregivers model positive behaviors with intention, they help children develop emotional regulation, empathy, responsibility, and resilience. Simply put, modeling lays the foundation for behavior transformation by showing children, not just telling them what to do.

Common Behaviors Children Mirror

1. **Emotional regulation**: yelling, sighing, deep breathing, or pausing
2. **Respect and language**: "please," "thank you," tone of voice
3. **Coping strategies**: taking a break, journaling, mindfulness
4. **Problem-solving**: asking for help, trying again, staying focused
5. **Responsibility**: cleaning up, following through, being honest

Modeling Strategies That Transform Behavior

1. **Model self-regulation out loud**

   Use language like, "I'm feeling frustrated, so I'm going to take a deep breath before I respond." Modeling helps children see regulation in action.

2. **Apologize**

   Own your mistakes. Say, "I shouldn't have raised my voice. I was upset, but I'm working on being calmer." Apologizing teaches accountability and humility.

3. **Practice what you preach**

   If you expect respect, show it. If you want calm voices, use one. Consistency between your words and actions builds trust and credibility.

4. **Narrate decision-making**

   Let children hear your internal problem-solving process: "I have two things I need to do. I'll do the hardest one first and get that one out of the way, and then I'll complete the easy one."

5. Show healthy emotional expression

Name your feelings and express them constructively: "I have a cold and am not feeling my best today. I might be quieter, have less patience, and be more irritable, but I'm still here for you."

6. Involve children in solutions

Invite them to observe and join in positive behavior: "Let's work together to figure out what to do when we feel overwhelmed."

Dr. Gwen's Tip, Tool, or Strategy:

Modeling isn't about being perfect or pretending to have all the answers. It's not about hiding mistakes or faking emotions to appear calm. True modeling involves being real, consistent, and intentional, not flawless. It doesn't mean adults must never get upset or make errors; instead, it's about showing how to handle those moments in healthy, constructive ways. Modeling isn't a one-time action or a scripted performance; it's an ongoing practice of aligning our behavior with the values and skills we want children to learn. When adults acknowledge their challenges and demonstrate how they work through them, they offer children a powerful and authentic example of growth and self-awareness. When it comes to behavior, your actions speak volumes. Every moment is an opportunity to model the kind of self-awareness, kindness, and self-regulation you want your children to carry into the world. Through consistent, mindful modeling, children can learn to rewrite their own behavior stories, one mirrored moment at a time.

N

Children

are likely to live

up to what

you believe of them.

~ Lady Bird Johnson

N – Nonverbal Cues

In the journey of transforming behavior, words matter, but so do the things we don't say. Children are expert observers. They notice the tightening of jaws, the rolling of eyes, sighs, and the crossing of arms. These nonverbal signals often speak louder than our verbal instructions. Understanding and becoming aware of our body language, tone, and facial expressions is essential when guiding a child from chaos to calm.

Nonverbals are often the first and most powerful form of communication children perceive. Long before children understand complex language, they are attuned to facial expressions, tone of voice, and body posture. These silent cues can either reinforce or contradict a message entirely. For example, saying "I'm not upset" through clenched teeth with a furrowed brow sends a confusing mixed message. Children often respond more to these unspoken cues than to what we actually say.

On the other hand, maintaining an open stance, making eye contact, and using a gentle tone can help de-escalate tension and build trust, even during moments of correction. Nonverbal cues also serve as a model; children mirror what they see. When adults consistently use calm, respectful nonverbal communication, they demonstrate emotional regulation, patience, and empathy, encouraging children to internalize and replicate those same behaviors.

Nonverbals are especially important for managing children with ADHD and autism because these children often process and interpret communication differently than their neurotypical peers. Children with ADHD may struggle with sustained attention and impulse control, making clear, calm nonverbal cues, such as pointing, gesturing, or using visual supports, is helpful in capturing their focus without overwhelming them with too many words. For children with autism, who may have difficulty interpreting tone or verbal instructions, consistent nonverbal signals can provide clarity and predictability. Visual structure, facial expressions, body posture, and proximity can all support understanding and reduce anxiety. Moreover, nonverbals help create a sense of safety and connection when words fail. A reassuring smile or a calm presence can speak volumes, assisting children to regulate and respond more effectively to expectations, requests, and directions. Using intentional nonverbal communication empowers caregivers and educators to support emotional and behavioral regulation in ways that are respectful, accessible, and supportive of the needs of individuals with neurodiversity. Here are some practical and commonly used nonverbal cues that parents, teachers, and caregivers can use to guide behavior, offer support, or reinforce expectations, especially helpful for children, including those with ADHD or autism:

Body Language
- Open arms or relaxed posture to show calm and safety
- Crossed arms or standing tall to convey a boundary or limit

- Squatting or sitting to get on a child's eye level (signals respect and connection)

Facial Expressions
- A smile to encourage or affirm
- Raised eyebrows to show surprise or prompt attention
- Calm, neutral face to de-escalate heightened emotions

Gestures
- Finger to lips for a quiet signal
- Thumbs up for approval or encouragement
- Hand over heart for appreciation
- Pointing to a visual schedule or a task as a redirection
- Palms facing down or out to signal "slow down" or "pause"

Visual Aids
- Picture cards to show emotions, choices, or expectations
- Traffic light cards (green = go, yellow = slow down, red = stop)
- Visual timers such as lava tubes or digital counters to support transitions or focus

Movement
- Walking slowly and calmly when approaching a dysregulated child. Hand-over-hand guidance for task initiation like writing (when appropriate)
- Stepping away briefly to model self-regulation or create space

Tone and Volume (Paraverbal cues)

- Gentle tone to soothe
- Lower volume to invite calm (children often mirror the speaker's volume)
- Pauses in speech to give time for processing and reduce overwhelming feelings.

Dr. Gwen's Tip, Tool, or Strategy:

One of the biggest mistakes adults make in behavior management is assuming that children automatically understand nonverbal cues, such as a raised eyebrow, crossed arms, or a stern look, without ever being explicitly taught what those signals mean. While adults often rely on these cues to communicate disapproval, urgency, or expectations, children, especially those who are younger or neurodivergent, may not accurately interpret them.

For example, A teacher may frown and point to a chair, expecting the student to sit down, but the child may feel confused or anxious instead of understanding the cue. A parent might cross their arms and sigh when their child doesn't follow directions, but the child may not link that body language to disappointment or concern. A teacher may stand or move close to a student to get them to stop talking or start working, but the child may not pick up on the cue.

When adults fail to explain their nonverbal messages, they miss opportunities to teach emotional literacy and foster shared understanding. By taking the time to narrate what their gestures or expressions mean ("When I raise my hand, it means stop talking and listen"), adults help children learn to read social cues and respond appropriately.

O

The sign of great parenting
is not the child's behavior.
The sign of truly great parenting
is the parent's behavior.
~ Andy Smithson

O – Observations

Before we can transform behavior, we must first understand it, and understanding begins with observation. Observation is more than just watching a child; it's the intentional act of noticing what's happening before, during, and after a behavior to identify patterns, triggers, and needs. In the chaos of busy classrooms or homes, it's easy to focus on correcting behavior in the moment. But when we slow down and pay close attention, we begin to see behavior for what it truly is: a form of communication.

Observations allow us to move beyond assumptions and truly understand the reasons behind a child's behavior. By carefully noticing what happens before, during, and after a behavior, adults can identify patterns, triggers, and unmet needs that might otherwise go unnoticed. Observation helps us distinguish between behavior that stems from skill deficits versus defiance, and it creates space for empathy and informed decision-making. Rather than reacting impulsively, observation empowers caregivers and educators to respond with intention, insight, and support. It's a foundational tool in transforming behavior, one that helps turn everyday moments into meaningful opportunities for growth, connection, and calm.

What to Observe

When observing, it's helpful to use the A-B-C format (Antecedent–Behavior–Consequence):

Antecedent – What happened before the behavior?

Behavior – What did the child do specifically?

Consequence – What happened after the behavior?

Other helpful things to notice include:

Who was present?

What was the child asked to do?

What was the emotional state of the child and the adult?

How did peers, siblings, or observers respond?

What environmental factors were present (noise, transitions, crowding, etc.)?

Tools for Effective Observation

1. **Behavior Logs**: Simple, structured forms to record A–B–C data and patterns.

2. **Frequency Charts**: Track how often a behavior occurs.

3. **Anecdotal Notes**: Brief, narrative descriptions of incidents for qualitative insight.

4. **Video Review** (if appropriate and with consent): A powerful tool to reflect on body language and triggers.

Just like the T.E.A.M.S. framework, observation works best when adults work together. Teachers, aides, counselors, support staff, and caregivers should share notes and observations to create a more comprehensive picture of the child's needs across various environments. Collaboration helps identify patterns that one person may miss. Observation is not passive; it's one of the most active and powerful tools we have for behavior transformation. By observing without judgment and documenting with care, we begin to understand the whole child, not just their outbursts or shutdowns. Observation is the process by which we transition from guessing to knowing, from reacting to responding, and from chaos to calm.

Dr. Gwen's Tip, Tool, or Strategy:

Sample Behavior Observation Form

Date: Wednesday, September 10, 2025

Observer's Name/Title: Ms. Jones, School Counselor

Student Name: (First) Jordan   **(Last)** Smith

Age: 6   **Grade:** 1st **Teacher:** Ms. Martin

Setting (location and activity): Ms. Martin 4th grade class during independent Math

Time of Observation (beginning and ending): 10:15 – 10:40 (25 minutes)

Antecedent (What happened before the behavior?): The teacher instructed the class to complete math problems 1 through 10.

Behavior (What did the child do?): Jordan began tapping his pencil loudly, humming, and turning around to talk to his peers.

Consequences (What happened after the behavior?): The teacher provided a nonverbal cue by walking over and standing by Jordan's desk. Jordan turned back around and stared at his Math paper. The teacher provided individual instructions and worked with Jordan on the first problem to ensure he understood the steps to take.

She told Jordan to complete the following three math problems and then raise his hand so she could check his work for accuracy before going on.

Notes/Comments: Jordan may benefit from preestablished nonverbal cues for redirection, allowing him the opportunity to ask questions if he doesn't understand what to do. If he starts working, the teacher can simply walk away. He may also benefit from having his assignments broken into manageable parts to help with attention and focus, as well as periodic check-ins to build his confidence in Math.

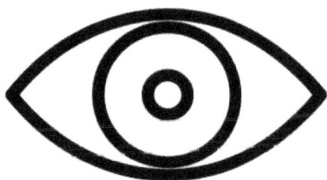

Observation is listening with your eyes.

~ Chris Richardson

P

Behind every young child
who believes in themselves
is a parent who believed first.

~ Matthew L. Jacobson

P – Positive Reinforcement

In the journey from chaos to calm, one of the most effective tools we can use is also one of the simplest: positive reinforcement. Children (and adults) thrive when their efforts, progress, and positive choices are recognized. Rather than focusing only on what went wrong, positive reinforcement shifts the spotlight to what's going right. It helps children feel seen for their strengths and motivated to repeat those behaviors. When used intentionally and consistently, it becomes a powerful strategy for shaping and sustaining desired behavior over time. Catch them being good!

Positive reinforcement is the practice of adding something pleasant or meaningful after a behavior to increase the likelihood that the behavior will happen again. Positive reinforcement can take many forms, including verbal praise, a tangible reward, extra playtime, a high-five, a fist pump, or a special privilege. The key is that the reinforcement is connected directly to the desired behavior and is meaningful to the child.

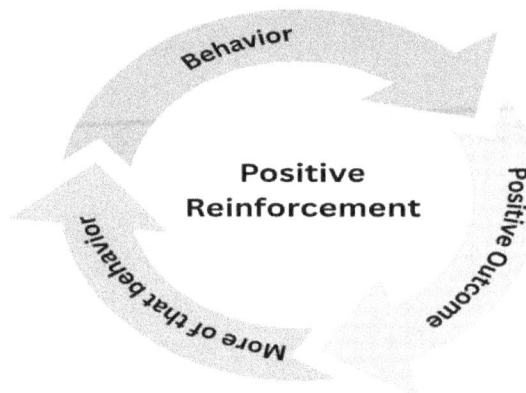

Behavior · Positive Outcome · More of that behavior · Positive Reinforcement

Why Positive Reinforcement Works

Children are wired to seek connection, approval, and success. When they experience a positive result from making a good choice, they begin to build internal motivation. Positive reinforcement works because it strengthens the connection between a desired behavior and a rewarding outcome, making it more likely that the behavior will happen again and again. When children experience praise, encouragement, or meaningful rewards after making positive choices, their brains associate those actions with a sense of accomplishment and well-being. This sense of accomplishment not only increases motivation but also builds trust between the child and the adult, reinforcing the idea that effort and good behavior are recognized and valued. Unlike punishment, which often focuses on what not to do, positive reinforcement teaches children what to do and why it matters, helping them internalize expectations and develop lasting habits of success. In short, it creates a feedback loop where effort is rewarded, leading to more effort and better behavior.

Types of Positive Reinforcement

- **Verbal**: "I noticed you cleaned up without being asked, thank you!"
- **Tangible**: Stickers, points, tokens, or small rewards
- **Privileges**: Extra recess, choice of game, being a helper
- **Social**: Applause, fist bumps, smiles, positive notes home

How to Use It Effectively

- **Be Specific**: Name the behavior you're reinforcing ("Great job using kind words when you were frustrated.")
- **Be Immediate**: Reinforce the behavior as soon as possible after it occurs.
- **Be Consistent**: Reinforce desired behaviors often, especially when building new habits.
- **Match the Child**: Choose reinforcers that are age-appropriate and meaningful to the individual child.

Dr. Gwen's Tip, Tool, or Strategy:

Positive reinforcement is not about spoiling children or avoiding accountability; it's about creating a climate where growth is recognized and encouraged. When children feel successful, they behave successfully. And when adults intentionally catch and celebrate those moments, even the smallest ones, they plant the seeds for long-term behavioral change. With consistency, clarity, and compassion, positive reinforcement becomes a cornerstone for transforming chaos into calm.

Common Mistakes to Avoid

- Using bribes. Positive reinforcement should not be a reward for compliance in the moment, but a consistent practice.
- Overusing. Using the same reinforcement repeatedly can reduce effectiveness.
- Reinforcing too late. The child may not connect the reward with the behavior.

- Ignoring effort. Even if the outcome isn't perfect, reinforce attempts toward positive behavior.

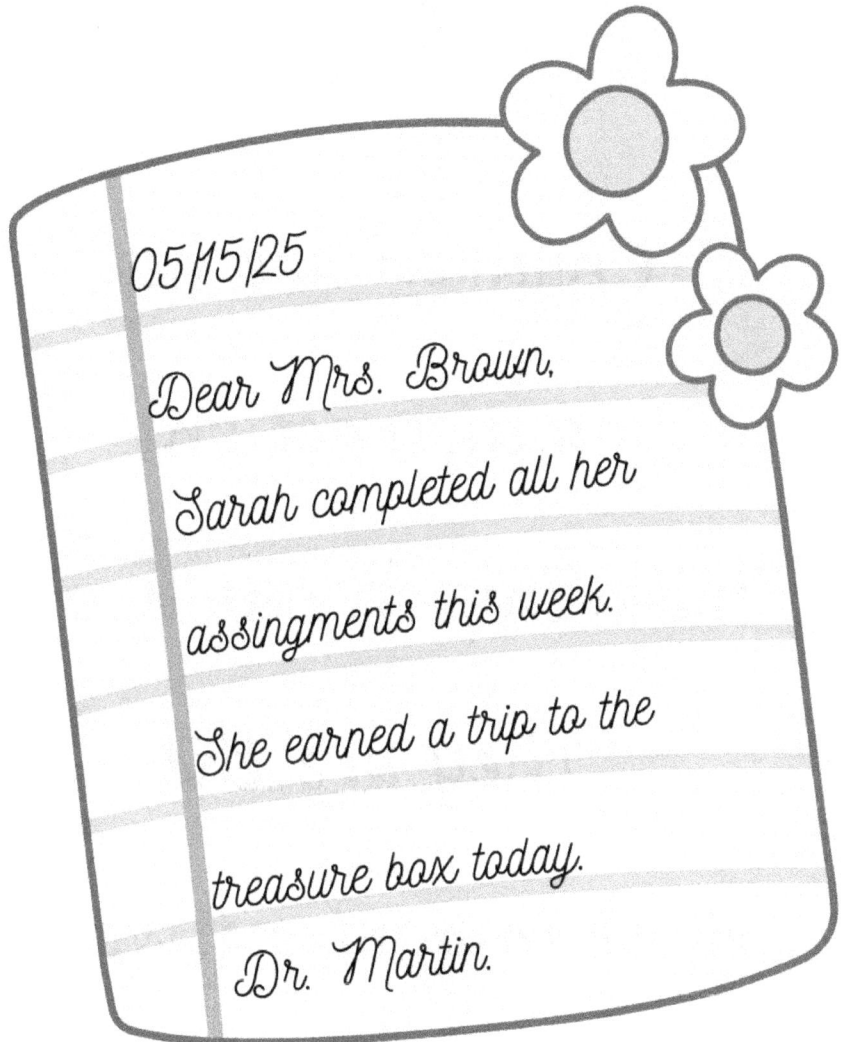

05/15/25

Dear Mrs. Brown,

Sarah completed all her

assingments this week.

She earned a trip to the

treasure box today.

Dr. Martin.

Q

Children are not

a distraction

from important work.

They are the

most important work.

— C.S. Lewis

Q – Quiet Time

Quiet time is a structured, intentional period during which children are given space to rest, reset, or reflect without external demands or overstimulation. It's not a punishment, it's a proactive strategy that supports emotional regulation, focus, and self-awareness. For many children, especially those who are easily overstimulated or emotionally reactive, quiet time can be a powerful alternative to reactive discipline.

Quiet time offers children a valuable opportunity to pause, reflect, and reset in a calm, low-pressure environment. It helps reduce overstimulation, allowing their minds and bodies to relax and recover from the day's demands. For children who experience emotional dysregulation, quiet time can provide a safe and consistent space to regain control, breathe, and process their feelings without external pressure. It promotes the development of self-soothing strategies and offers an opportunity for them to build awareness of their emotions and needs. Incorporating quiet time into daily routines not only supports emotional and behavioral growth but also helps prevent outbursts by giving children the tools and space to manage stress before it escalates.

Calm down corners in the classroom and at home provide children with a designated, supportive space to manage big feelings and regain emotional control. These intentional areas are not meant to isolate or punish, but to empower children by offering tools and comfort items, such as breathing visuals, sensory objects, books, or calming prompts, that help them self-regulate. In classrooms, calming corners contribute to a positive learning environment by reducing disruptions and teaching students to manage their emotions constructively. At home, they foster consistency and reinforce the idea that it's okay to take a break when overwhelmed. Over time, children learn to recognize their emotional cues and use the space proactively, which builds independence, resilience, and emotional intelligence.

What Quiet Time Might Look Like
- A designated cozy or calm-down corner
- Soft lighting, headphones, or sensory items
- Access to a feelings journal, drawing materials, or a favorite book
- Timed (5–15 minutes, depending on age) with a gentle transition back to activity if they don't return on their own
- Optional: use of a timer, calm visuals, or soft background music

When to Use Quiet Time
- After a challenging emotional moment
- As part of a daily routine (e.g., post-lunch, mid-morning, after recess or specials)
- Before or after difficult transitions
- When a child requests space
- To prevent escalation when early signs of dysregulation are present

Dr. Gwen's Tip, Tool, or Strategy

Here's a list of soothing, sensory, and supportive items that can be included in a Calm Down Corner, whether at school or home, to help children regulate their emotions and return to a calm state.

Suggestions for a Calm Down Corner

Comfort Items

- Soft pillows or a small beanbag chair
- Cozy blanket or weighted lap pad
- Stuffed animals or calming plush toys

Creative Tools

- Crayons, markers, and coloring books
- Scratch paper or a feelings journal
- Calm-down cards or mood check-in sheets

Sensory Tools

- Fidget toys (e.g., stress balls, pop-its, putty, monkey noodle)
- Visual timers or glitter jars
- Noise-canceling headphones or soft music
- Sensory bottles or calming lights (like lava tubes, lamps, or LEDs)

Visual Supports

- Calm breathing visuals (e.g., square breathing, balloon breathing, box breathing, ocean breathing)
- Emotion identification charts, or "feelings faces"

- Social Stories (e.g., I can use helpful hands and walking feet.)

Self-Regulation Tools

- Mirror (for practicing facial expressions and breathing)
- Choice cards for calming activities
- Mini routine or checklist ("1. Breathe 2. Stretch 3. Rejoin")

Optional Additions

- Books about emotions and mindfulness
- Aromatherapy (safely used, like scented stickers or diffusers)
- Small puzzles or quiet tactile games
- Sand tray

find your own Path

R

The beautiful thing

about learning

is that no one

can take it

away from you.

— B.B. King

R – Restorative Practices

Restorative practices are relationship-centered approaches that focus on repairing harm, rebuilding trust, and fostering accountability when behavior breaks down or conflict occurs. Instead of relying on punishment, these practices emphasize open communication, empathy, and collaborative problem-solving. Children are guided to reflect on their actions, understand the impact on others, and take meaningful steps to make things right. Restorative practices are effective because they address the root causes of behavior, teach essential emotional and social skills, and reinforce the idea that everyone plays a role in maintaining a respectful and caring environment. By shifting the focus from control to connection, restorative practices help transform behavior while strengthening relationships, both essential to moving from chaos to calm.

Restorative Tools and Approaches

- **Restorative Conversations**: Guided one-on-one or small group dialogues using reflective questions
- **Repair Circles**: Structured group discussions for peer conflict or community harm
- **Reflection Forms or Journals**: Written tools to explore impact, feelings, and next steps
- **Apology and Action Plans**: Combines a verbal apology with a specific plan to rectify the situation.

Restorative Questions for Children

- What happened?
- What were you thinking and feeling at the time?
- Who was affected and how?
- What do you need to feel better?
- What can you do to repair the harm?

Restorative Conversation Example

Context: A student (Sam) became frustrated during group work and shouted at a peer, disrupting the class.

Teacher: Sam, thank you for sitting down with me. I want to discuss what happened earlier in a calm manner so we can move forward together. Are you ready to talk?

Sam: Yeah... I guess so.

Teacher: Let's start with your side. What happened during group time?

Sam: They weren't listening to my ideas. I got mad and yelled at them.

Teacher: Thanks for being honest. What were you thinking or feeling at that moment?

Sam: I felt like no one cared what I had to say. I was trying to help, but they ignored me.

Teacher: That sounds frustrating. When we feel ignored, it's easy to get upset. How do you think your reaction, yelling, affected your group?

Sam: I think it made them mad. And it stopped everything.

Teacher: You're right. It also made it more difficult for everyone to complete the project. What do you think you can do to make things right with your group?

Sam: I could say sorry. And maybe ask if we can try again.

Teacher: That's a great idea. Saying sorry and asking to restart shows leadership. What can you do next time you start to feel frustrated?

Sam: Maybe take a break or ask for help.

Teacher: Perfect. I'll be here to support you with that. Let's talk to your group together so we can reset and finish strong.

Dr. Gwen's Tip Tool or Strategy:

Restorative Practices in Action

Restorative practices are about healing, not hurting. When children have the opportunity to make things right in a safe and supportive way, they learn some of the most essential life skills: empathy, communication, and responsibility. In both home and school environments, these practices turn moments of chaos into opportunities for deeper connection, stronger relationships, and lasting behavior change.

- **In the classroom**: After a conflict, two students engage in an open discussion to share their perspectives and agree on next steps.

- **At home:** A child who yelled at a sibling writes a reflection and helps repair the relationship by playing a game together, hugging it out, writing an apology note, or simply saying they are sorry for yelling.

Never ruin an apology
with an excuse.
~ Benjamin Franklin

S

Be the change

that you wish

to see in the world.

— Mahatma Gandhi

S – Structured Routines

When chaos feels constant, structure becomes the anchor. Children thrive in environments where they feel grounded and know what to expect. Structured routines provide a sense of safety, consistency, and clarity that supports emotional regulation and reduces behavioral challenges. They reduce anxiety by minimizing the unknown, allowing children to focus more on learning and less on wondering what's coming next. Consistent routines teach time management, promote independence, and establish expectations without needing constant reminders. When routines are predictable, children can anticipate transitions and make smoother behavioral adjustments. This section examines how predictable routines transform uncertainty into stability, enabling children to shift from reactive to responsive behavior.

For children with ADHD, autism, trauma histories, or anxiety, structured routines are essential. Predictability supports nervous system regulation, reduces meltdowns, and fosters trust in the adults who provide stability and consistency.

Structured routines reduce the number of decisions a child has to make in the moment, making it easier to stay regulated. They provide behavioral cues without needing constant adult redirection. We all know how hectic and chaotic the morning can be. As a special education teacher, every day started with 15 minutes of journal writing. This reflective calming activity resulted in fewer morning outbursts because children knew what to expect and felt welcomed and centered. Journaling was especially beneficial for resource students entering the class at various times throughout the day, as it minimized disruptions and provided a calm-down activity during transitions.

What Makes a Routine "Structured"?

A structured routine is:

- Consistent: Happens the same way each time.
- Clear: Steps are broken down and communicated clearly, either visually or verbally.
- Developmentally appropriate: Matches the child's ability and needs.
- Flexible when needed: Offers gentle transitions or options within boundaries.

Examples of Effective Routines

- Morning Routine: Wake up → Brush teeth → Get dressed → Eat breakfast → Pack backpack → Leave for school
- Classroom Transition Routine: 5-minute warning → Visual cue → Clear desk → Line up quietly
- Bedtime Routine: Bath → Pajamas → Reading → Gratitude reflection → Lights out

Routines are the rhythm of a calm environment. They help children build trust, gain confidence, and practice responsibility in predictable, manageable steps. While every day may not be perfect, a well-established routine offers a safety net that helps children bounce back from disruptions and gives adults the structure they need to guide with clarity and care.

Dr. Gwen's Tip, Tool, or Strategy:

Routines are most effective when they are developmentally appropriate, flexible, and tailored to the unique needs of each child and family. While the structure provides a helpful framework, routines are not one-size-fits-all. A routine that works well for a 5-year-old will likely look very different from one designed for a 12-year-old. Younger children may need more guidance, visual supports, and built-in play or rest periods, while older children may benefit from increased independence, choice, and input in the routine itself.

Other factors, such as neurodiversity, trauma history, mental health challenges, cultural practices, or family work schedules, can also influence how routines are created and carried out. For example, a child with ADHD may require tasks broken into manageable parts and visual timers to support their focus. In contrast, a child who experiences anxiety may benefit from calming activities woven throughout the day.

It's essential for families to treat routines as living tools that can be adjusted over time. The goal is not rigid perfection, but consistency with compassion. When routines are responsive to a family's values, rhythms, and needs, they become a source of connection, regulation, and predictability, key ingredients in transitioning from chaos to calm.

After-School to Bedtime Routine Example

3:00 PM – Arrive Home & Transition

- Take off your shoes and backpack
- Unpack the lunchbox and folder
- Quick emotional check-in or hug

3:15 PM – Snack & Hydration

- Healthy snack and drink
- Light conversation or 10 minutes of quiet decompression

3:30 PM – Homework/Study Time

- Focused work session (20–40 minutes, depending on age)
- Include short movement or "brain breaks" as needed
- Place your homework in your backpack in the proper place.

4:15 PM – Free Time or Play

- Screen time, outdoor play, reading, or creative activity
- Unstructured but calm, not overly stimulating

5:30 PM – Dinner & Family Time

- Eat together and share "highs and lows" of the day
- Help set or clear the table

6:15 PM – Evening Responsibilities

- Pack your lunch for tomorrow
- Set out next day's clothes
- Chores (room or play area tidy-up)

7:00 PM — Bath Time

- Bath or shower, brush teeth, and put on pajamas

7:20 PM — Calming Activity

- Reading, coloring, journaling, or a quiet family game
- Gentle music or deep breathing exercise, if needed

7:45 PM — Bedtime Connection

- Share one thing they're proud of or grateful for
- Cuddle or brief conversation about tomorrow

8:00 PM — Lights Out

- Same bedtime each night helps regulate sleep
- Use a night light or white noise if needed

T

Education is not

the filling of a pail,

but the lighting of a fire.

- William Butler Yeats

T – Token Economy

When a child is stuck in cycles of misbehavior, motivation can become a major challenge. Token economies are one way to reignite that motivation and help children connect effort with reward. Far from being a system of bribery, a well-structured token economy teaches responsibility, delayed gratification, and goal setting in a clear and empowering manner. When used thoughtfully, it becomes a bridge from chaotic behavior to calm, intentional choices.

A token economy is a behavior reinforcement system in which children earn tokens (e.g., stickers, points, or physical tokens) for demonstrating desired behaviors. These tokens can later be exchanged for predetermined rewards or privileges. This system makes abstract behavioral expectations more concrete, providing children with visual, tangible evidence of their progress.

Token economies work because they provide children with clear, immediate feedback that links their behavior to positive outcomes in a tangible way. By earning tokens for specific, desired actions, children begin to understand that their choices have power and that consistent effort is noticed and valued. This system breaks down larger behavioral goals into manageable steps, making progress feel achievable and motivating. Token economies also teach essential life skills such as delayed gratification, goal setting, and self-monitoring. For children who struggle with impulse control, attention, or emotional regulation, the visual and structured nature of a token system offers a sense of power and predictability, two key ingredients for behavioral growth and transformation.

Steps to Set Up a Token Economy

1. Define Target Behaviors

Choose 1–2 clear, age-appropriate behaviors to focus on (e.g., "keep hands to self," "complete morning routine," "use calm words").

2. Select Tokens

Use something visible and trackable, such as stars, stickers, poker chips, points on a board, or digital apps.

3. Choose Rewards

Create a menu of meaningful, realistic incentives that vary in "cost," with some small and frequent, and others larger and earned over time.

4. Establish Rules

- How many tokens can be earned?
- How are they tracked?
- When and how can they be exchanged?

5. Model and Launch

Practice the system with your child. Praise effort and explain how tokens are connected to behavior.

6. Review and Adjust

Regularly revisit the system. Make adjustments if the child loses interest in rewards or shows significant improvement in behavior.

Dr. Gwen's Self-Care Tip, Tool or Strategy:

Example: Classroom Token Economy

Target Behavior: Complete the Independent Reading Assignment

Token: Plastic coins in a clear jar

Rewards:

3 tokens = Sit by a friend

5 tokens = 10 minutes of free time

10 tokens = Treasure box

Avoiding Common Pitfalls

1. **Don't overcomplicate it**

   Keep it simple and focused.

2. **Don't withhold earned tokens**

   Once earned, tokens should not be taken away.

3. **Don't use it forever**

   Token systems should fade away gradually as behavior improves and becomes internalized.

4. **Avoid rewarding only the outcome**

   Recognize effort and progress, too.

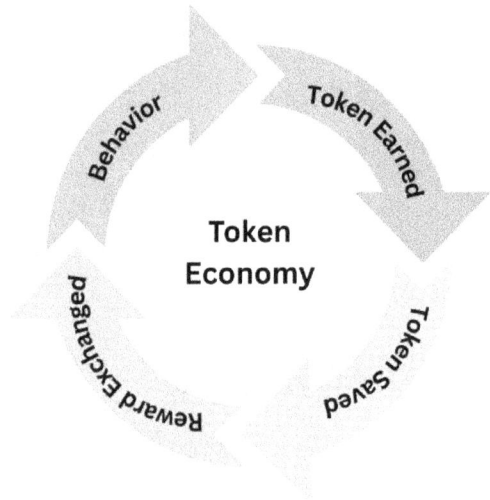

(diagram: Token Economy cycle — Behavior → Token Earned → Token Saved → Reward Exchanged)

U

Too often we give children answers to remember rather than problems to solve.

~ Roger Lewin

U – Understanding Triggers

Before we can help children change their behavior, we must understand what is causing it. In many cases, what appears to be "bad behavior" is actually a reaction to a trigger, a person, place, event, or internal state that sets off a strong emotional or behavioral response. By learning to recognize and respond to these triggers with empathy and strategy, we stop treating behavior like a mystery and start guiding children with intention and insight.

A trigger is anything, internal or external, that activates a child's nervous system and causes them to feel overwhelmed, unsafe, anxious, angry, or out of control. Triggers vary from child to child and may not always be evident to the adults around them. For children, especially those who are neurodivergent or have experienced trauma, even small changes in routine or tone of voice can be enough to trigger a behavioral response.

Common Triggers in Children

- Sensory overload (bright lights, loud sounds, scratchy clothes).
- Unpredictable changes in routine or expectations.
- Feeling misunderstood or not heard.
- Social dynamics (peer rejection, teasing, feeling left out).
- Perfectionism or fear of failure
- Transitions between activities or settings.
- Being hungry, tired, or sick
- Experiences tied to past trauma or loss

How to Identify a Child's Triggers

1. Observe patterns: When does the behavior usually occur?
2. Track the ABCs: What happens Before (Antecedent), During (Behavior), and After (Consequence)?
3. Ask the child: Use age-appropriate reflection tools or questions.
4. Talk to caregivers: Triggers at home may differ from school.
5. Consider the environment: Look at noise, lighting, group size, and demands.

Dr. Gwen's Tip, Tool, or Strategy:

When we understand what triggers a child's behavior, we stop reacting to symptoms and start responding to **causes**. Identifying triggers gives us, and the child, greater clarity, compassion, and control. Instead of blaming children for melting down, we start asking, "Why?" By anticipating and supporting them through their triggers, we provide them with the tools to regulate, recover, and ultimately rise with resilience.

Strategies for Managing Triggers

1. Prepare and preview: Use visuals, schedules, and countdowns to facilitate smooth transitions.
2. Offer choices: Control can reduce anxiety and resistance.
3. Use calming strategies proactively: Practice deep breathing, utilize sensory tools, and take movement breaks.

4. Create safe spaces: Calm corners where children can go before they lose control.

5. Build coping skills: Teach children to identify and express their feelings and encourage them to ask for help when needed.

6. Reinforce success: Acknowledge when a child manages a known trigger with self-control and self-regulation.

Too Loud
Make It Stop

V

A child seldom

needs a good

talking to as

much as a

good listening to.

— *Robert Brault*

V – Validation

When a child is struggling with behavior, our first instinct is often to correct or redirect. But before change can happen, connection must come first. Validation is the foundation of that connection. It's the practice of acknowledging and accepting a child's thoughts, feelings, or experiences, even when their behavior requires attention. Validation doesn't mean approval of the behavior; it means **recognition** of the why behind it. When children feel seen and understood, they are more open to reflection, learning, and transformation.

Validation helps children feel seen, heard, and emotionally safe, especially during moments of distress or behavioral challenges. When adults take the time to acknowledge a child's feelings without judgment or dismissal, it sends the message that their emotions are real and that it's okay to express them. Validation fosters trust and connection, which are essential for providing meaningful guidance and promoting growth. Rather than escalating the situation, validation helps calm the nervous system and opens the door for problem-solving and self-regulation. It doesn't excuse misbehavior; it creates the foundation for understanding and changing it.

Examples of Validating Responses

1. Instead of saying: "Stop crying, it's not a big deal." Try: "It looks like you're feeling sad. How can I help?"

2. Instead of saying: "Why are you so angry over something so small?"

   Try: "I can tell you're frustrated. Let's take a minute to figure this out together."

3. Instead of saying: "There's no reason to be scared." Try: "That seems scary to you. You're not alone. I'm right here."

Dr. Gwen's Self-Care Tip:

Behavior is communication, and when children act out, what they often need most is to feel seen, heard, and understood. Validation is the emotional anchor that helps them return to a calm state. It teaches children that their feelings matter and that they can manage those feelings with support and guidance. When we validate before we redirect, we transform chaos into connection, and from there, real behavior change can begin.

Validation doesn't mean letting go of boundaries or expectations. In fact, it helps children accept redirection more calmly when they feel heard first.

For example: "I understand that you're mad and wanted to keep playing. It's time to clean up, let me help you."

This approach builds cooperation through empathy rather than power struggles.

How to Practice Validation

1. **Pause and listen** – Give the child your attention

2. **Reflect** – Name what you observe ("You seem upset...")

3. **Normalize the Emotion** – "It's okay to feel that way."

4. **Avoid Judgment or Dismissal** – Focus on connection, not correction.

5. **Follow with Support** – "What do you need right now?" or "Let's work through this together."

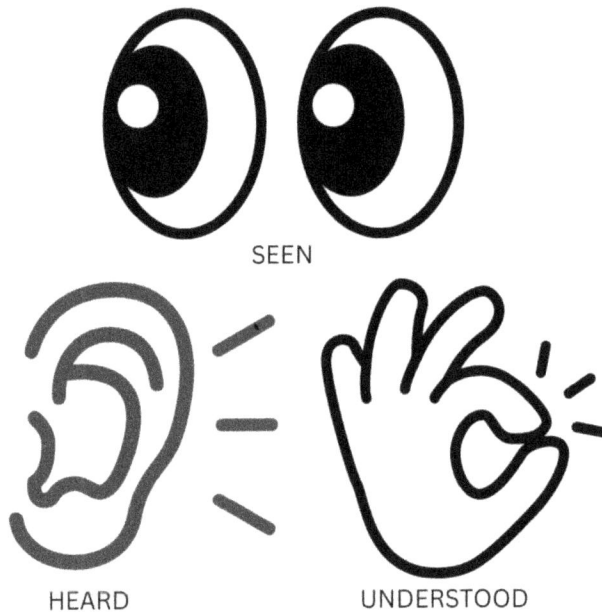

SEEN

HEARD   UNDERSTOOD

W

Believe in your child so strongly that the world can't help but believe in them, too.

— *Unknown*

W – Warning Signs

Children rarely go from calm to crisis without giving clues along the way. These clues, known as warning signs, are the subtle or obvious signals that a child is beginning to struggle emotionally or behaviorally. When adults learn to recognize and respond to these early indicators, they can prevent escalation, support regulation, and create a safer and more responsive environment. Recognizing warning signs is a key step in transforming chaos into calm.

Warning signs are the physical, verbal, emotional, or behavioral cues that signal a child is becoming dysregulated. They're like the emotional "check engine" light, letting us know that something is going on beneath the surface. These signs may be unique to each child and can change depending on the setting, time of day, or emotional triggers.

Recognizing warning signs allows adults to intervene early, before a child enters a complete meltdown or aggressive outburst. Early intervention helps children feel understood and supported, and it teaches them to identify their signs of stress. Over time, this awareness leads to stronger emotional regulation skills and fewer behavior challenges.

Understanding a child's warning signs is like learning their emotional language. When we notice the build-up instead of waiting for the breakdown, we create space for healing, safety, and skill-building. Instead of reacting with frustration, we respond with care, and in that response, the transformation from chaos to calm begins.

Common Warning Signs in Children

Physical Signs:

- Tense muscles or clenched fists
- Restlessness or pacing
- Rapid breathing or a flushed face
- Fidgeting or rocking

Verbal Signs:

- Voice getting louder or sharper
- Negative self-talk ("I'm stupid," "Nobody likes me")
- Repeating the exact words or questions (broken record)
- Arguing, whining, or talking back

Emotional Signs:

- Withdrawing or shutting down
- Crying or quick mood swings
- Overreacting to small problems
- Increased anxiety or clinginess

Behavioral Signs:

- Refusal to follow directions
- Avoiding tasks or trying to escape
- Aggression toward objects or people
- Sudden impulsive or risky behavior

Dr. Gwen's Tip, Tool, or Strategy:

Teaching children to recognize their **own** warning signs empowers them to better understand and manage their emotions before they become overwhelming. By helping children tune into how their body feels, what thoughts they're having, or how their behavior changes when they're upset, we give them the tools to catch themselves earlier and choose healthier coping strategies. Using visuals like feeling charts, "body check" worksheets, or personal signal lists can make this process concrete and age-appropriate. Over time, children begin to connect the dots between their inner experiences and outward actions, allowing them to pause, reflect, and respond rather than react, an essential skill for lifelong emotional regulation.

What Adults Can Do

1. Observe patterns during high-stress times or settings.
2. Stay calm and use a regulated tone and body language.
3. Offer choices or calming tools (such as breathing exercises, fidgets, or space).
4. Validate feelings without escalating the situation.
5. Redirect gently toward a regulation strategy or a safe break.
6. Debrief later when the child is calm to build insight.

X

It takes courage

to grow up

and become

who you really are.

~ E.E. Cummings

X – eXpectation Mapping

One of the most common causes of misbehavior is misunderstanding. When children don't know what's expected of them, or the expectations keep changing, they're more likely to act out, shut down, or resist. Just as a GPS provides step-by-step directions, expectation mapping gives children a mental roadmap for behavior, helping them stay on track and feel more confident along the way.

Expectation mapping is a visual or verbal guide that breaks down what appropriate behavior looks like in specific settings, situations, or routines. It helps children prepare for transitions, understand their role, and anticipate what's coming next. By clearly defining expectations in advance, we reduce confusion and increase success by providing children with clear, consistent guidance on how to behave in specific situations. Instead of relying on assumptions or vague instructions, children are given a concrete "map" that outlines what success looks like, step by step. Maps reduce anxiety, increase confidence, and give them the tools to self-monitor and stay on track. It also promotes fairness and consistency, so children understand that expectations remain constant from one moment to the next. When children know exactly what's expected, they're more likely to meet those expectations, turning uncertainty into clarity and chaos into calm.

Examples of Expectation Mapping

Morning Routine at School

- Unpack your bag and turn in your homework.
- Complete journal writing.
- Start morning work quietly.
- Raise your hand for help.
- Greet classmates quietly and respectfully.
- Complete a quiet activity until the whole group lesson begins (e.g., catch up on incomplete assignments, read a book, go to the puzzle table, draw, do a word search, etc.).

Homework Time at Home:

- Choose a quiet workspace.
- Gather materials before starting.
- Work for 15-20 minutes, then take a short 3–5-minute break.
- Ask for help if you get stuck, don't give up.

Before a Field Trip:

- Listen to adult directions.
- Stay with your group.
- Use an inside voice on the bus.
- Keep your hands and feet to yourself.

Visual Option: Create a checklist or cartoon sequence showing expected behaviors.

Dr. Gwen's Tip, Tool, or Strategy:

Children thrive when they know what's expected of them and how to meet those expectations. Expectation mapping is a simple yet powerful tool for reducing conflict, supporting independence, and creating calm, predictable environments. When we make expectations consistent, visible, understandable, and achievable, we empower children to rise to them, and in doing so, we pave the way for lasting behavioral transformation.

Tips for Success

1. Keep expectations developmentally appropriate and realistic.
2. Use first-person phrasing when possible ("I keep my hands to myself").
3. Be consistent across caregivers and settings.
4. Allow children to reflect on their progress: "Which expectation did I follow well today?" "What do I need to improve tomorrow?"

Y

Encouragement is oxygen

for the soul.

Say YES

to uplifting words.

~ George M. Adams

Y – YES/NO Decision Making

Children thrive on structure and clarity, but too many choices, or unclear ones, can quickly lead to power struggles, shutdowns, or defiance. Yes/No Decision-Making is a straightforward strategy that enables children to navigate boundaries with confidence, reduces power struggles, and fosters a sense of predictability, which in turn helps children feel safe and in control. Instead of overwhelming them with open-ended questions or vague directions, adults offer clear, manageable options that empower children to choose within limits, thereby minimizing the likelihood of becoming overwhelmed or defiant. This practice helps restore order, builds self-regulation, and reinforces that choices have natural consequences, both positive and negative.

Yes/No decision-making is a boundary-based approach to choices. It involves giving children clearly defined options, framed in "yes" or "no" terms, to help them take ownership of their behavior. It eliminates confusion and helps prevent bargaining, stalling, or arguing. It's not about being controlled, it's about providing a simple, safe structure in moments of emotional intensity or uncertainty. With consistency, Yes/No decision-making becomes a powerful tool for calming chaos and teaching responsibility.

Dr. Gwen's Tip, Tool, or Strategy:

Yes/No decision-making provides the structure children need to feel secure and the autonomy they crave to feel empowered. By making boundaries clear and choices consistent, we reduce emotional chaos and guide behavior with confidence. In the process, we teach children that their decisions matter and that every choice shapes their path forward.

Things to Remember

- Stay calm and factual.
- Don't negotiate once a yes/no choice has been presented.
- Follow through consistently on outcomes.
- Always offer choices that are developmentally appropriate and within your control.
- Frame "no" as a natural response to behavior, not as a punishment.

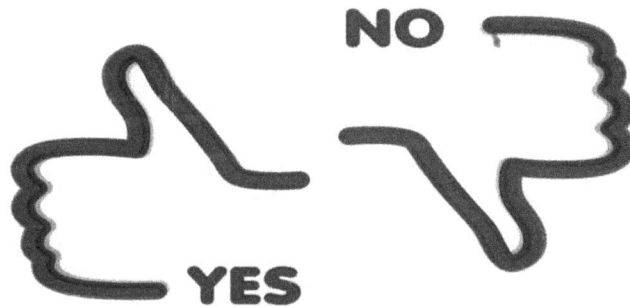

Z

It is not what you
do for your children,
but what you have taught them
to do for themselves that will
make them successful human
beings.

~ Ann Landers

Z – Zones of Regulation

Before children can change their behavior, they first need to recognize how they feel. The Zones of Regulation is a widely used framework that helps children identify their emotional states and learn tools to manage them. Developed by occupational therapist Leah Kuypers, this color-coded model breaks complex emotions into four simple "zones" that children can easily understand and relate to. Using the Zones helps move kids from emotional confusion to clarity, paving the way for calm, constructive behavior.

The framework includes **four color-coded zones**, each representing a different level of alertness or emotional state:

Blue Zone: Low energy states — sad, tired, bored, sick

Green Zone: Calm and focused — happy, ready to learn, in control

Yellow Zone: Elevated emotions — worried, frustrated, silly, excited

Red Zone: Intense states — angry, out of control, overwhelmed, panicked

These zones are not "good" or "bad"; they are all normal. The key is helping children recognize which zone they're in and what tools they can use to either stay regulated or return to a calm state.

The Zones of Regulation work because they simplify the complex world of emotions into four easy-to-understand categories, making it easier for children to recognize and communicate how they're feeling. By using colors instead of labels like "good" or "bad," the Zones remove shame and judgment, encouraging emotional honesty and self-reflection. This approach helps children develop the language and awareness they need to manage their emotions before they escalate into disruptive behavior. Over time, children learn that feelings are normal and manageable, and they begin to build a personal toolbox of strategies to return to a regulated, calm state. The visual, consistent structure of the Zones provides both children and adults with a shared language to transition from chaos to clarity.

Zones and Autism

The Zones of Regulation are especially effective for children on the autism spectrum because they provide a clear, visual, and structured way to identify and manage emotions, skills that can be challenging due to difficulties with emotional recognition, communication, and self-regulation. The use of color-coded zones simplifies abstract feelings into something concrete and predictable, reducing confusion and anxiety. For many autistic children, routines and visual supports are essential tools, and the Zones framework naturally aligns with those strengths. It also encourages consistent language and cues across home, school, and therapy settings, fostering a supportive and unified approach. By making emotions more accessible and regulation more achievable, the Zones empower children on the spectrum to better navigate social situations, transitions, and daily challenges.

Zones and ADHD and Oppositional Defiance Disorder (ADHD/ODD)

The Zones of Regulation are highly effective for children with ADHD and ODD because they offer a structured, nonjudgmental approach to understanding and managing emotions, areas that are often challenging for both groups. Children with ADHD benefit from the visual and predictable format of the Zones, which helps them pause, notice their feelings, and choose appropriate coping strategies before acting impulsively. The framework supports their development of executive functioning skills and provides clear tools for emotional regulation. For children with ODD, the Zones reduce power struggles by shifting the focus from control to self-awareness. Instead of framing behavior as "bad," the Zones encourage children to reflect on how they're feeling and what they need to get back to a regulated state. Zones empowers them to take responsibility for their actions without feeling shamed or forced. In both cases, the Zones offer a shared emotional language that fosters trust, improves communication, and builds confidence, laying the foundation for more consistent and calm behavior over time.

Dr. Gwen's Tip, Tool, or Strategy:

How to Use the Zones

1. **Introduce the Concept**

   Use visuals, posters, or stories to explain each zone in child-friendly terms.

2. **Identify the Zones**

   Help children connect real-life feelings to zones ("When I lost the game, I was in the red zone.")

3. **Build a Toolbox**

   Work with the child to create a list of calming strategies for each zone (e.g., deep breaths in yellow, stretch or talk in red, take a break in blue).

4. **Use Daily Check-Ins**

   Ask, "What zone are you in right now?" at different points in the day.

5. **Model and Practice**

   Share your zones with the child ("I'm in the yellow zone right now, so I'm going to take a breath before I speak.")

AFTERWARDS

As you reach the final pages of From Chaos to Calm, I hope this book has served as more than just a guide; it has been a companion, a reminder, and encouragement that transforming behavior is not about perfection, but about progress. Whether you're a parent, teacher, or counselor, your role in a child's life is powerful and deeply impactful. Every strategy you've explored, every reflection you've made, and every tool you've tried is part of building a foundation for growth, regulation, and connection.

Behavior transformation doesn't happen overnight. It takes time, patience, and the willingness to pause, reset, and try again. There will be hard days. However, there will also be moments of breakthrough when a child uses words instead of outbursts, when they reflect rather than react, when they choose calm over chaos. Celebrate those wins. Honor **your** efforts. And know that with each intentional choice you make, you're helping to shape not just behavior, but confidence, compassion, and resilience.

Remember, calm isn't the absence of noise or emotion; it's the presence of safety, understanding, and consistency. Thank you for being part of that calm for the children in your care.

If this book has supported your journey, I'd be honored if you could leave a review on Amazon or my website. Your feedback helps others find these tools and join the movement toward intentional, heart-centered behavior support. You can also find additional self-care resources like the D.E.A.R Journal, additional A to Z guides, games, card decks, and more for children and adults at www.DrGwensCounselorCafe.com.

Let's stay connected through social media by following **Dr. Gwen's Counselor Cafe** on Facebook, Instagram, LinkedIn, and YouTube for new tools, encouragement, and upcoming releases.

Let's keep growing together.

With gratitude,

Dr. Gwen
Dr. Gwen's Counselor Cafe LLC

Reflections

AWARENESS, GROWTH, GOALS

This section is an opportunity to write what you learned about yourself, growth opportunities, and future goals.

My Commitment

Make a commitment to yourself on how you will continue to transform behavior at work or home. Writing your commitment down and sharing it with someone will make it more achievable and you more accountable. Afterward, take the behavior management pledge.

Chaos to Calm Pledge

I pledge to guide children with patience, empathy, and purpose. I will model calm, respectful behavior and communicate expectations clearly and consistently. I will see the child behind the behavior and respond with care, celebrating both effort and outcomes. I will create safe spaces for reflection and growth, and when things feel chaotic, I will remain calm, so they can, too.

Signed _____

The behavior management checkup on the next page is designed to help parents, teachers, and caregivers reflect on their current behavior management practices, identify strengths, areas for improvement, and growth opportunities. Use it as a self-assessment, team discussion guide, or planning tool during professional development or parent meetings.

How to Use:

1. **Read each question thoughtfully**

   Consider how often and consistently each practice is used in your current environment, such as at home, in the classroom, or a counseling setting.

2. **Rate yourself**

3. **Reflect on patterns**

   Highlight or make notes next to areas of strength or those areas that need improvement.

4. **Choose 1-2 action steps**

   Based on your responses, select small, specific goals to work on over the next week or month (e.g., "Post visual expectations near the door" or "Introduce a calm-down space").

5. **Repeat regularly**

   Use this tool quarterly or as needed to track growth, refresh strategies and support positive behavior transformation.

Chaos to Calm Check Up

		YES	NO
1.	Are expectations clearly communicated to children?		
2.	Do you consistently model calm and respectful behavior?		
3.	Are behavior expectations visual and accessible (e.g., posters, routines, schedules)?		
4.	Do you respond to behavior with consistency and follow through?		
5.	Are children given regular opportunities to regulate themselves (e.g., taking breaks, using a calm-down corner)?		
6.	Do you employ proactive strategies, such as yes-or-no decision-making and nonverbal cues?		
7.	Are triggers and warning signs being tracked and addressed?		
8.	Are reinforcement systems (praise, tokens, incentives) used regularly?		
9.	Do children have a voice and ownership in behavior plans or goals?		
10.	Is reflection and repair encouraged after conflict or misbehavior?		

Acknowledgements

Writing From Chaos to Calm has been both a labor of love and a reflection of the many children, families, and educators who have shared their stories, struggles, and successes with me over the years. I am deeply grateful for every child who challenged me to think differently, every parent who trusted me with their child's growth, and every educator, especially my educational aides, who worked tirelessly alongside me to support students through the most challenging moments.

To my colleagues in counseling, education, and behavioral health, you continue to inspire me with your passion, resilience, and commitment to helping children thrive. Your voices and perspectives helped shape this book into a practical, compassionate guide.

To my loving husband, family, and friends, thank you for your patience, encouragement, and unwavering support throughout the editing and creative brainstorming sessions. You kept me grounded and reminded me of the why behind this work, and you also reminded me to give myself grace during those times when I needed to take a step back.

To the self-care community that surrounds Dr. Gwen's Counselor Café LLC, your belief in the importance of mental health and emotional wellness fuels everything I create. Thank you for being part of this journey and for helping me share this message with the world.

And most importantly, to every adult who picks up this book intending to do better, not just for the children in their care, but for themselves, you are the calm in the chaos. Thank you for being here.

Dr. Gwen

Book Review

1. What inspired you to read this book?

2. What chapter or section was most helpful to you, and why?

3. Did you find the A to Z format engaging and easy to follow?

   ☐ Yes   ☐ Somewhat   ☐ No

   Please explain: _____

4. Which tool, strategy, or worksheet do you see yourself using most?

5. How has this book changed the way you approach behavior in children?

6. Were the examples and language clear and relatable?

   ☐ Very clear   ☐ Somewhat clear   ☐ Confusing at times Comments:

   _____

7. Would you recommend this book to others?

   ☐ Yes   ☐ Maybe   ☐ No

8. What additional topics or tools would you like to see in future resources?

9. Have you followed Dr. Gwen's Counselor Cafe on social media for more tips and tools?

   ☐ Yes   ☐ Not yet — but I plan to!   ☐ No

10. Is there anything you'd like to say to the author?

Quotations

Quotations in this book were obtained from compilation websites. Although every precaution has been taken to verify the accuracy of the quotes, some may contain errors or have been misattributed. The author and publisher assume no responsibility or liability for any errors or omissions, nor the use and application of any of the contents of this book.

References

Center on the Social and Emotional Foundations for Early Learning (CSEFEL). (n.d.). Teaching Your Child About Feelings. Retrieved from http://csefel.vanderbilt.edu

Cooper, J. O., Heron, T. E., & Heward, W. L. (2020). *Applied Behavior Analysis* (3rd ed.). Pearson.

Delahooke, M. (2019). *Beyond behaviors: Using brain science and compassion to understand and solve children's behavioral challenges.* PESI Publishing & Media.

Greene, R. W. (2016). *Raising human beings: Creating a collaborative partnership with your child.* Scribner.

Gulchak, D. J., & Lopes, J. A. (2022). Self-management interventions for reducing challenging behaviors: A systematic review. *Campbell Systematic Reviews,* 18(1), e1234.

Hanley, G. P., Jin, C. S., Vanselow, N. R., & Hanratty, L. A. (2020). Producing meaningful improvements in problem behavior of children with autism via synthesized analysis and skill-based treatment. *Behavior Analysis in Practice,* 13(1), 52–60. https://doi.org/10.1007/s40617-019-00356-2

Horner, R. H., Sugai, G., & Anderson, C. M. (2020). Examining the evidence base for school-wide positive behavior support. *Focus on Exceptional Children, 52*(6), 1–15. https://doi.org/10.17161/fec.v52i6.15852

Kutscher, M. L. (2014). *Kids in the syndrome mix of ADHD, LD, autism spectrum, Tourette's, anxiety, and more!* (2nd ed.). Jessica Kingsley Publishers.

Kuypers, L. (2011). The Zones of Regulation. San Jose, CA: Social Thinking Publishing.

Markham, L. (2012). *Peaceful parent, happy kids: How to stop yelling and start connecting.* Tarcher Perigee.

Nelsen, J. (2019). *Positive discipline: The classic guide to helping children develop self-discipline, responsibility, cooperation, and problem-solving skills.* Harmony.

National Association of School Psychologists. (2021). Functional Behavior Assessment: A Problem-Solving Model. https://www.nasponline.org

Raver, C. C. (2002). Emotions matter: Making the case for the role of young children's emotional development for early school readiness. *Social Policy Report, 16*(3), 3–19.

Riden, B. S., Kumm, S., & Maggin, D. M. (2021). Evidence-based behavior management strategies for students with or at risk of EBD: A mega review of the literature. *Behavioral Disorders, 46*(4), 243–256.

Siegel, D. J., & Bryson, T. P. (2018). *The yes brain: How to cultivate courage, curiosity, and resilience in your child.* Bantam Books.

Smith, R. G., & Iwata, B. A. (2021). Functional Analysis Methodology: Refinements and Applications. *Journal of Applied Behavior Analysis, 54*(1), 5–21. https://doi.org/10.1002/jaba.733

Dr. Gwen's Counselor Café LLC

Children Resources

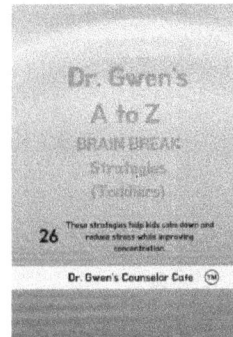

I CARE BINGO
DR. GWEN'S COUNSELOR CAFE LLC

Dr. Gwen's A to Z Plan de Estrategias de Afrontamiento
Estas estrategias ayudan a los niños a calmarse y reducir el estrés mientras mejoran la concentración.
26
Dr. Gwen's Counselor Cafe

Dr. Gwen's A to Z COPING STRATEGIES GAME PLAN
These strategies help kids calm down and reduce stress while improving concentration.
26
Dr. Gwen's Counselor Cafe

Dr. Gwen's A to Z Soluciones para Descansos para Niños Pequeños
26 Estas estrategias ayudan a los niños a calmarse y reducir el estrés mientras mejoran la concentración.
Dr. Gwen's Counselor Cafe LLC

Dr. Gwen's A to Z BRAIN BREAK Strategies (Toddlers)
26 These strategies help kids calm down and reduce stress while improving concentration.
Dr. Gwen's Counselor Cafe

Dr. Gwen's A TO Z SELF-CARE GUIDE for Teens

Dr. Gwen's A TO Z SELF-CARE GUIDE for Teens
SMILE, SHINE, SHARE

Live Your BEST LIFE
5-MINUTE SELF-CARE JOURNAL

Adult
Resources

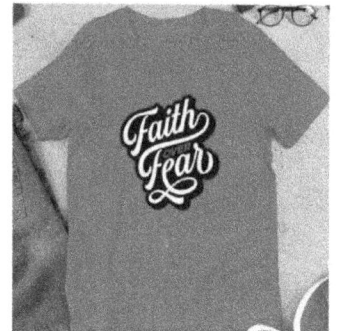

~ Notes ~

~ Notes ~

~ Notes ~

~ Notes ~

www.ingramcontent.com/pod-product-compliance
Lightning Source LLC
Chambersburg PA
CBHW062045090426
42740CB00016B/3022